DISABILITY AND THE DISABLED – ISSUES, LAWS AND PROGRAMS SERIES

CREATING LIVABLE COMMUNITIES FOR PEOPLE WITH DISABILITIES

DISABILITY AND THE DISABLED – ISSUES, LAWS AND PROGRAMS SERIES

Creating Livable Communites for People with Disabilities
Alise Vanags
2010. ISBN: 978-1-60741-534-3

DISABILITY AND THE DISABLED – ISSUES, LAWS AND PROGRAMS SERIES

CREATING LIVABLE COMMUNITIES FOR PEOPLE WITH DISABILITIES

ALISE VANAGS
EDITOR

Nova Science Publishers, Inc.
New York

LIBRARY OF CONGRESS CATALOGING-IN-PUBLICATION DATA
Creating livable communities for people with disabilities / editor, Alise Vanags.
p. ; cm.
Includes bibliographical references and index.
ISBN 978-1-60741-534-3 (hardcover)
1. People with disabilities--Services for--United States. I. Vanags, Alise. II. National Council on Disability (U.S.)
[DNLM: 1. Community Health Services--organization & administration--United States. 2. City Planning--methods--United States. 3. Disabled Persons--rehabilitation--United States. 4. Environment Design--United States. 5. Residence Characteristics--United States. WA 546 AA1 C912 2009]
HV1553.C74 2009
362.4'0485--dc22 2009031703

Published by Nova Science Publishers, Inc. ✦ New York

CONTENTS

PREFACE

Creating Livable Communities is an outgrowth of the National Council on Disability's (NCD) interest and recent work in the topic of livable communities for people with disabilities. The main impetus for this interest is threefold: 1) the prospect of a growing population of people with disabilities as the baby boom generation ages, 2) the desire that people with disabilities—indeed, all people-have to live in their own homes and communities and maintain their self-determination, dignity, and independence for as long as possible, and 3) the pressures that these factors will exert on local communities that strive to become livable for people of all ages and abilities. This book thoroughly examines these challenges, as well as addresses promising practices.

This book consists of public domain documents, a National Council on Disability Report, Creating Livable Communites, dated October 31, 2006, which have been located, gathered, combined, reformatted, and enhanced with a subject index, selectively edited and bound to provide easy access.

Executive Summary

Creating Livable Communities is an outgrowth of the National Council on Disability's (NCD) interest and recent work in the topic of livable communities for people with disabilities. The main impetus for this interest is threefold: 1) the prospect of a growing population of people with disabilities as the baby boom generation ages, 2) the desire that people with disabilities—indeed, *all* people—have to live in their own homes and communities and maintain their self-determination, dignity, and independence for as long as possible, and 3) the pressures that these factors will exert on local communities that strive to become livable for people of all ages and abilities. Two research reports recently published by NCD thoroughly examine these challenges, as well as promising practices in addressing them: *Livable Communities for Adults with Disabilities* (2004) and *The State of 21st Century Long-Term Services and Supports: Financing and Systems Reform for Americans with Disabilities* (2005). The findings in these reports motivated NCD to delve deeper into the topic of livable communities, identify barriers to developing them, and shed light on potential methods for overcoming these barriers.

Disability prevalence is rising in the under-age-65 population and, although it has decreased slightly for people aged 65 and older, it will begin to rise sharply as the current senior population of 34 million doubles over the next 20 years.[1] In light of these demographic developments, communities will face significant challenges as they strive to address consumers' needs in a coordinated and comprehensive manner, reduce fragmentation in the service delivery system, provide consumer choice, and implement policies and programs that help adults with disabilities remain independent and involved in community life.

As the findings from the two reports mentioned above suggest, *collaboration and coordination among federal agencies, as well as between these agencies and the states,* can support communities as they build and sustain key elements of livability.

Creating Livable Communities presents *six strategies or policy levers,* gleaned from the two previous research reports, that can be implemented on the federal and local levels to promote collaboration and coordination and support livable community objectives. Each of these strategies is illustrated by actual promising practices at both the federal and state levels that can be adapted and replicated elsewhere. It should be noted that these general policy levers and specific illustrative examples were selected from a vast array of actions that can be taken to address the various elements of community livability.

DEFINITION OF A LIVABLE COMMUNITY

The definition of "livable community" used here is derived from the National Council on Disability's earlier report entitled *Livable Communities for Adults with Disabilities:*

A livable community:

- Provides affordable, appropriate, accessible housing
- Ensures accessible, affordable, reliable, safe transportation
- Adjusts the physical environment for inclusiveness and accessibility
- Provides work, volunteer, and education opportunities
- Ensures access to key health and support services
- Encourages participation in civic, cultural, social, and recreational activities

Within each of these six areas, a livable community strives to maximize people's independence, assure safety and security, promote inclusiveness, and provide choice.

While no one community in the United States has addressed all six of these livability goals to equal degrees, many states, counties, and local communities have made extraordinary improvements in their livability for people with disabilities in one or even several of these areas. Their experiences and achievements can serve as inspiration and provide replicable "best practices," which other communities can emulate as they strive to become more livable.[2]

SIX STRATEGIES TO IMPROVE COMMUNITY LIVABILITY

Strategy One: Agreement on Changes in the Collection and Management of and Access to, Multiple Agency Information about Programs and Benefits in Order to Be Consumer Responsive

As the examples in this section illustrate, this strategy can help ensure that older people and people with disabilities have access to key health and supportive services that enable them to continue living in the community as independently as possible.

Examples

- Aging and Disability Resource Centers (ADRC) are community-based centers that centralize information about long-term support options in the community. ADRC programs provide information and assistance to both public and private pay individuals and serve as the entry point to publicly administered long-term supports, including those funded under Medicaid, the Older Americans Act, and state programs.
- 2-1-1 is a phone number designated by the Federal Communications Commission to be used exclusively for community information and referral purposes. There are 157 active 2-1-1 systems in 32 states that provide consumers with centralized information and referral to basic human needs resources; physical and mental health resources; employment support; support for older people and people with disabilities; as well as support for children, among other services.

Strategy Two: Utilization of Favorable Tax Treatment (E.G. Tax Credits) to Stimulate Change in Individual and Corporate Behavior That Encourages Investment in Livable Community Objectives

The availability of appropriate and affordable housing choices is one of the most important measures of community livability. As the examples below illustrate, Strategy Two can be used to expand such housing opportunities for people with low incomes and/or people with disabilities and ensure that the housing is affordable and accessible.

Examples

- The Low Income Housing Tax Credit provides states with a financial "carrot" to encourage development of housing without having to allocate direct federal expenditures. It is a significant source of financing for developers seeking to construct and rehabilitate housing for people with disabilities.
- The Kentucky Housing Corporation (KHC) is Kentucky's state housing finance agency that administers and monitors a number of federal and state affordable housing programs and sets state policy on housing. One of its objectives is to build partnerships with state and local housing agencies to ensure that new housing is fully accessible and incorporates universal design principles. The KHC has developed universal design requirements that are mandatory for any projects that receive a certain amount of debt or subsidy financing from the Corporation. It also provides technical assistance to developers to ensure they are meeting all building requirements, including the universal design guidelines, and inspects and certifies buildings once they are built.

Strategy Three: Agreement on Common Performance Measures across Multiple Federally Funded Programs

There is an enormous variety of programs that are designed to help older people and people with disabilities live independently in the community. But how effective are these programs? Do they respond to people's actual needs and support their aspirations? Strategy Three is one way to begin addressing these questions. The initiatives illustrating this approach include developed tools that facilitate measurement of performance and outcomes. These tools can be applied to a variety of programs that serve people with disabilities and older people.

Examples

- The Program Assessment Rating Tool (PART) was developed by the Office of Management and Budget to assess and improve program performance so that Federal Government programs can achieve better results. PART reviews help identify the various strengths and weaknesses of federal programs to inform funding and management decisions aimed at making the programs more effective.
- The Administration on Aging (AoA), an agency within the U.S. Department of Health and Human Services, is collaborating with more than 20 states to develop standardized performance outcome measures and data collection instruments to evaluate programs funded by the AoA, such as congregate nutrition programs, information and assistance, and transportation services. In addition, the Federal Interagency Forum on Aging Related Statistics is a group of 11 collaborating agencies that has established a set of key indicators that describe the status of the U.S. population aged 65 and older.

Strategy Four: Utilization of Private Sector Match to Competitively Secure Public Funding and Stimulate Public-Private Sector Partnerships

Livable communities ensure that all residents, regardless of ability, are able to participate in the community's economic, civic, and social life. The examples included under Strategy Four illustrate how public-private sector partnerships can promote asset development and financial independence among people with low incomes and people with disabilities. When people with low incomes and people with disabilities are able to accumulate income to continue their education, buy homes, and/or start businesses, they not only enrich their own lives, they help support the economy of the communities in which they live.

Examples

- Individual Development Accounts (IDAs) are "asset development tools," one of many economic development programs created by

Congress to provide savings incentives among selected populations. It is a successful policy mechanism that has helped thousands of people who are low-income wage earners build their personal assets, live independently, and contribute to their communities' economy in the same ways that millions of other citizens do.

- Iowa is one of the many states that has passed IDA legislation in ways that minimize restrictions and facilitate program delivery. Iowa was one of the first states to pass IDA policy as part of its sweeping welfare reform bill. The five-year program, called Iowans Save!, has created thousands of IDAs for individuals with low incomes, including people with disabilities.

Strategy Five: Agreement on Changes in Infrastructure to Consolidate Administration of Multiple Programs and Improve Ease of Access

Livable communities provide residents with access to employment opportunities and transportation options. But access to employment and transportation—which are inextricably linked—is among the most vexing barriers that people with disabilities face, partly because of lack of coordination among the various agencies and programs involved. The examples in Strategy Five illustrate how consolidation and coordination can improve access to these key livable community objectives.

Examples

- The Workforce Investment Act (WIA) was passed by Congress in 1998 to better serve job seekers with and without disabilities as well as employers through a new framework that brings together multiple federal employment and training programs into a unified system of support. The single system is anchored by comprehensive One-Stop centers in each workforce investment area in all fifty states. While WIA allows states and local governments the authority to design how best to implement the One-Stop system, the guiding principles of the Act require a focus on streamlined and integrated service with an emphasis on improved coordination and collaboration across agency lines.
- United We Ride (UWR) is a relatively new program that provides information, technical assistance, and grants to states to develop and

implement comprehensive action plans for coordinating human service transportation to make it more cost-effective, accountable, and responsive to consumers who are "transportation disadvantaged." UWR promotes education and outreach to transportation providers and consumers; consolidation of programs; reduction of restrictive and duplicative laws, regulations, and programs; and coordinated planning.

Strategy Six: Utilization of Waiver Authority to Promote State Options to Advance Consumer Choice and Community Participation

The primary objective of the livable community concept is to provide people with disabilities choice and support to live independently in the community. The examples in Strategy Six illustrate long-term services and supports policies that support this objective. Many people believe that long-term services and supports alternatives like state Medicaid waiver programs should be the rule rather than the exception.

Examples

- Medicaid and Social Security offer two important sources of funding for support of individuals with disabilities. Over the past 25 years, significant expansion of Medicaid has occurred through the creation of waiver authority, which allows states to apply to the Centers for Medicare and Medicaid Services for approval of different amendments to their state plans that may impact who is eligible for services, what services may be covered, and the limits of coverage. Similarly, the Social Security Administration (SSA) has waiver authority it can grant to states on a case-by-case basis to modify existing policies and procedures and encourage testing alternative policies and procedures that promote independence and self-sufficiency for individuals with disabilities and their families. These current waiver programs constitute the principal way that states can offer services and supports that are consumer-centered and promote independence and community participation among people with disabilities.
- Maryland's New Directions Program, the Florida Freedom Initiative, and California Independence Plus are examples of state waiver

programs that are rebalancing Medicaid's original institutional bias and, instead, are providing self-directed home and community based services with expanded control by and flexibility for people with disabilities and low-income older people, enabling them to remain in their own homes and communities for as long as possible. The Florida Freedom Initiative also includes an SSA waiver to increase asset limits. The results are producing enhanced consumer choices and satisfaction.

RECOMMENDATIONS FOR ACTION

The selected strategies and examples in this report offer possibilities to change the way government organizes and manages resources, interacts with the business community and community developers, and responds to the expectations of evolving consumer interests, needs, and preferences for more choice and control in the delivery of support services. The recommendations for action included in the report offer multiple, complementary options for the legislative and executive branches of the Federal Government as well as states to proactively adopt strategies and policy levers that invest in livable community outcomes. With the aging of America and the challenges of disability in over 20 percent of families nationwide today, and possibly a greater percentage tomorrow, it is vital to focus on knowledge utilization and transfer from best practice examples.

Recommendation 1

Issue a new Executive Order to charge the Office on Disability of the Department of Health and Human Services to chair a time-limited workgroup (six months, for example) on livable communities that would adopt and promote the strategies in this report. The workgroup would include representatives of the Departments of Housing and Urban Development (HUD), Transportation, Education, Labor, and Treasury, the Social Security Administration, the Centers for Medicare and Medicaid Services, the Administration on Aging, the Administration on Developmental Disabilities, and the Office of Community Services within the Department of Health and Human Services.

Recommendation 2

Modify federal requirements for allocation of low-income housing tax credits so that, in making awards to developers, all states require a) the adoption of universal design standards, and b) documentation of approaches to allow a minimum of ten percent of units in multifamily affordable housing developments to be affordable to individuals with disabilities on fixed incomes (i.e. SSI/SSDI recipients).

Recommendation 3

Modify current performance measures being used to assess individual program strengths and weaknesses to focus on cross department and agency collaboration to enhance livable community outcomes.

Recommendation 4

Utilize grant funds from the Centers for Medicare and Medicaid Services, Social Security Administration, and Departments of Labor, Commerce, Health and Human Services, Transportation, and Housing to offer a consolidated Livable Communities Program Initiative that streamlines 1) a single application for funds, 2) utilization of waiver authority, 3) consolidation of program management and service delivery, and 4) use of tax credits to reengineer the delivery of long-term supports, transportation, housing, employment, education, and cultural, social, and recreational opportunities at a community level.

Recommendation 5

Expand tax incentives to promote matched savings plans for low-income wage earners across the life span.

Recommendation 6

Utilize and leverage community service opportunities and volunteers to support livable community objectives.

Recommendation 7

Focus on the Gulf Coast recovery and rebuilding to promote livable community outcomes.

Recommendation 8

Establish a National Resource Center on Livable Communities to educate policymakers, government administrators, community developers, people with disabilities, and the public about best practices in policy development and program implementation.

The recent Hurricane Katrina and Rita disasters demonstrated that lack of cooperation and coordination at all levels of government can have disastrous effects on people of all walks of life, particularly those who are among the most vulnerable. These events and their aftermath bring a new sense of urgency to the need to promote cooperation and coordination among agencies as well as adoption of livable community principles for the benefit of all Americans.

End Notes

[1] National Council on Disability. (2005). *The State of 21st Century Long-Term Services and Supports: Financing and Systems Reform for Americans with Disabilities*, p.15. Washington, DC. Available at: http://www.ncd.gov/newsroom/publications/2005/publications.htm

[2] National Council on Disability. (2004). *Livable Communities for Adults with Disabilities*. Washington, DC. Available at: http://www.ncd.gov/newsroom/publications/2004/LivableCommunities.htm#executivesummary

In: Creating Livable Communities for People... ISBN: 978-1-60741-534-3
Editor: Alise Vanags

Chapter 1

INTRODUCTION

National Council on Disability

BACKGROUND

In the past two years, the National Council on Disability (NCD) has published two groundbreaking research reports that have elucidated the elements that make communities livable for people with disabilities, barriers to developing livable communities, and strategies to overcome these barriers.

Published in December 2004, the first report, *Livable Communities for Adults with Disabilities,* identifies:

1. The key elements of communities that promote the health, well being, and independence of adults with disabilities, or at risk of developing disabilities, across the age spectrum. These elements include:
   Providing affordable, appropriate, accessible housing
   Ensuring accessible, affordable, reliable, safe transportation
   Adjusting the physical environment for inclusiveness and accessibility
   Providing work, volunteer, and education opportunities
   Ensuring access to key health and support services
   Encouraging participation in civic, cultural, social, and recreational activities
2. Communities that have incorporated one or more of these elements into their physical, social, and service systems and the strategies and interventions they have employed to do so,

3. The major challenges and barriers that communities face in moving toward greater livability for persons with disabilities, as well as factors that facilitate positive change, and
4. Promising policy levers and policy changes that, if adopted, would facilitate communities' capacity to enhance their livability for their residents.

Published in December 2005, the second report, *The State of 21st Century Long-Term Services and Supports: Financing and Systems Reform for Americans with Disabilities,* is an in-depth examination of the current status of long-term services and supports (LTSS) for people with disabilities and contains recommendations for reducing the fragmented nature of service and support delivery systems. The report points out that:

1. There is a lack of a coherent public policy regarding national long-term services and supports for people with disabilities
2. Service and support delivery systems are fragmented, with uneven access and service provisions
3. There are more than 20 federal agencies and almost 200 programs that provide a wide range of assistance and services to people with disabilities, yet no single federal program, agency, or congressional committee has responsibility for the management, funding, and oversight of LTSS
4. The current LTSS system is funded primarily by state and federal programs, but there is no portability provision across states and usually no single entry point at the community level for individuals with disabilities and seniors to learn about and access service and support options
5. The costs of LTSS, which make up 22 percent or more of state budgets, are becoming unsustainable, and there is need for systems reform

While these two reports focus on different, though closely related, topics—the first on *livable communities*, the second on *community-based long-term services and supports* for people with disabilities—they come to many of the same conclusions about what people with disabilities want and need in order to live as independently as possible, for as long as possible, in the community. For example, both reports note that:

1. People with disabilities, like *all* people, want to live in supportive communities that facilitate their independence, help them maintain self-determination, and integrate them fully into community life
2. People with disabilities desire and deserve choices, whether they are seeking health and support services, transportation or housing options, work and education opportunities, or civic, social, or recreational activities
3. In the health and supportive services arena, people's desire for independence and control is more likely to be satisfied when health care systems a) are consumer directed, b) provide care coordination, c) allow "money to follow the person" to eliminate barriers to care and provide consumers with choice over the location and type of services provided, d) provide high-quality, seamless, consumer-centered, and continuous care across settings and providers, and e) provide support services that are linked to housing to increase the availability and efficiency of service provision
4. People with disabilities and their caregivers need and want access to timely, understandable, and culturally appropriate information that helps them navigate through the maze of health care, supportive services, housing, transportation, and other systems and make informed choices

Both reports also point out that there are considerable barriers to fulfilling these desires and needs. They note, for example, that:

- Coherent, comprehensive federal policies are lacking, leading to fragmentation in service and support delivery systems and frustration for people with disabilities and their caregivers
- Scant resources or funding "silos" that restrict how funds can be used contribute to the fragmentation of these systems
- Multiple, disparate resources frequently overlap and other times leave big gaps in service
- Accountability and quality control are hampered by lack of uniform performance measures across systems and programs
- Access to information is made unnecessarily difficult because it is neither centralized nor shared among agencies
- Collaboration among agencies is more the exception than the rule

As a result of this work, NCD was motivated to examine these barriers further and identify strategies, policy levers, and promising practices that will inspire and demonstrate the value of multiple agency collaboration at both the federal and state levels in order to achieve livable community objectives. This is in keeping with NCD's overall purpose to promote policies, programs, practices, and procedures that guarantee equal opportunity for all individuals with disabilities and to empower individuals with disabilities to achieve economic productivity, independent living, inclusion, and integration into all aspects of society.

STRATEGIES TO PROMOTE COOPERATION AND COLLABORATION AND RECOMMENDATIONS FOR ACTION

The two NCD reports mentioned above identified a set of six strategies or policy levers that can be applied at the federal and state levels to facilitate much-needed cooperation and collaboration among agencies. *Creating Livable Communities* presents these six strategies, each illustrated with in-depth reviews of selected federal and state programs that have been or are being successfully implemented for the benefit of people with disabilities. Each of these examples addresses one or more livable community objectives, including access to information, affordable and accessible housing, work, education, transportation, and appropriate health and long-term services and supports. These strategies and "promising practice" examples are ones that can be adapted or replicated in other contexts.

In addition to these six strategies and "on the ground" examples of federal and state programs that are actually addressing and/or overcoming barriers to building livable communities, we present eight recommendations to stimulate action in the legislative and executive branches of the Federal Government to further the livable community agenda and improve quality of life for people with disabilities and their families.

In 2005, in the aftermath of Hurricanes Katrina and Rita, the nation witnessed the sad consequences of the lack of cooperation and coordination among federal, state, and local agencies that were responsible for evacuating people who lived in the path of the storm and resettling them. Not surprisingly, the most vulnerable residents of the affected areas—people with disabilities and older people, particularly those in hospitals and nursing homes—were among those who suffered the most during and after the storm. These unfortunate events reminds the nation that we need to redouble our efforts to remove the barriers that prevent agencies at all levels from working together to safeguard our citizens and communities as well as support independent living among people with disabilities and promote their inclusion in all aspects of society.

In: Creating Livable Communities for People... ISBN: 978-1-60741-534-3
Editor: Alise Vanags

Chapter 2

Strategy One: Agreement on Changes in the Collection and Management of and Access to, Multiple Agency Information about Programs and Benefits in Order to Be Consumer Responsive

National Council on Disability

As the examples in this section illustrate, this strategy can help ensure that older people and people with disabilities have access to key health and supportive services that enable them to continue living in the community as independently as possible.

Aging and Disability Resource Centers

Long-term service and support systems in many states are fragmented and disjointed, with many public and private programs and services delivered by a variety of agencies and organizations. The navigation of the long-term services and support system can be confusing and frustrating for older people and people with disabilities of all ages and their family members. The Aging and Disability Resource Center grant program (ADRC) was established to pilot new approaches to interagency coordination that improve access and the availability of information to meet the needs of the target populations.

The ADRC program is part of the President's New Freedom Initiative, which aims at overcoming barriers to community living for people of all ages with disabilities. The ADRC program is the collaborative effort of the U.S. Department of Health and Human Services' Administration on Aging (AoA) and the Centers for Medicare and Medicaid Services (CMS). The ADRC program takes an important step towards meeting AoA's vision for long-term services and supports:

- Affordable choices and options that promote independence and dignity for individuals
- Consumer control and meaningful involvement in the design and delivery of the programs and services that affect their lives
- Information that empowers people to make informed decisions
- Easy access to a range of health, long-term services, and environmental supports
- Support for family caregivers
- Assurances that people are receiving the highest quality care available

Ready access to consolidated information and referral services helps make communities more livable for residents of all ages and abilities.

Background

ADRC programs provide information and assistance to both public and private pay individuals and serve as the entry point to publicly administered long-term supports including those funded under Medicaid, the Older Americans Act, and state revenue programs.

History

Research into the delivery of long-term support services revealed many troubling facts. Long-term support services are sustained by numerous funding streams, administered by multiple agencies, and have complex, fragmented, and often duplicative intake, assessment, and eligibility functions. People who qualify for publicly-funded supports are often frustrated by the complexity of the system and its disconnected points of entry and different rules of eligibility. Individuals are often channeled towards skilled nursing facilities without being made aware of other available supports that may assist them in remaining in the community.

ADRCs were established to help consumers overcome these problems by providing "one-stop shopping" for information, counseling, and access on all long-term support programs and services. Resource Centers will also improve the states' ability to manage public resources and monitor program quality through centralized data collection and evaluation.

Target Population for Assistance

States must target ADRC services to the elderly population and at least one additional population (*i.e.,* individuals with physical disabilities, serious mental illness, and/or mental retardation/developmental disabilities).

ADRC programs serve individuals who need long-term support, their family caregivers, and those planning for future long-term support needs, regardless of income. The Centers also serve as a resource for health and long-term services and supports professionals and others who provide services to the elderly and to people with disabilities.

Location of ADRCs

ADRCs are presently in operation in these 43 states and in Guam, the District of Columbia, and the Northern Mariana Islands:

2003 ADRC Grantees	2004 ADRC Grantees
Louisiana	Alaska
Maine	Arkansas
Maryland	California
Massachusetts	Commonwealth of the Northern Mariana Islands
Minnesota	Florida
Montana	Georgia
New Hampshire	Illinois
New Jersey	Indiana
Pennsylvania	Iowa
Rhode Island	New Mexico
South Carolina	North Carolina
West Virginia	Wisconsin
2005 ADRC Grantees	
Alabama	
Arizona	
Colorado	
District of Columbia	
Guam	

Table (Continued)

2005 ADRC Grantees
Hawaii Idaho Kansas Kentucky Michigan Mississippi Nevada Ohio Tennessee Texas Vermont Virginia Washington Wyoming

Stakeholder Involvement

Stakeholders are involved in the planning, implementation, and evaluation of ADRCs. Most ADRCs follow AoA and CMS's recommendation to include stakeholders from the following list:

Area Agencies on Aging	State Health Insurance Assistance Programs (SHIPs)	State Assistive Technology Act Projects (AT Act Projects)
Consumer advocacy groups and organizations	Long-term services and supports Ombudsman Programs	Housing authorities
Benefit Planning Assistance and Outreach (BPAO) programs funded by the Social Security Administration	Developmental Disabilities Councils	Volunteer groups
One-Stop Centers and other efforts funded by the Department of Labor	State Mental Health Planning Councils	Employers
Alzheimer's Association chapters	Independent Living Centers	Faith-based service providers
State Vocational Rehabilitation entities	Community service providers	Private philanthropic organizations
	Other community-based organizations	

In addition, states operating ADRCs establish or designate an Advisory Board to assist in the development and implementation of their program and advise the lead state agency on: (a) the design and operation of Resource Centers; (b) stakeholder input; (c) the state's progress toward achieving the goal and vision for ADRCs; and (d) other program and policy development issues related to the state's Resource Center program.

Services Offered

As an information clearinghouse, the ADRCs offer advice and assistance to individuals with disabilities across the age spectrum as well as to physicians, hospital discharge planners, and other professionals who work with older people or people with disabilities. Services offered through the single entry point can be grouped into six areas:

1. **Information and Assistance.** Provide information to the general public about services, resources, and programs in areas such as: disability and long-term related services and living arrangements, health and behavioral health, adult protective services, employment and training for people with disabilities, home maintenance, nutrition, and family care.

2. **Long-Term Services and Supports Counseling.** Offer objective information, consultation, and advice about the options available to meet an individual's long-term services and supports needs.

3. **Benefits Counseling.** Provide accurate and current information on private and government benefits and programs.

4. **Emergency Response.** Ensure that people are connected with someone who will respond to urgent situations that might put someone at risk, such as a sudden loss of a caregiver.

5. **Prevention and Early Intervention.** Promote effective prevention efforts to keep people healthy and independent and offer both information and intervention activities that focus on reducing the risk of disabilities.

6. **Access to Family Care Benefit.** Administer the long-term services and supports Functional Screen to assess the individual's level of need for services and eligibility for the Family Care benefit.

Resources

Former Secretary of Health and Human Services, Tommy Thompson, announced the funding of 12 state grants to develop ADRCs in September of 2003. Twelve additional ADRC grants were announced in April of 2004. Eighteen states and Guam were funded in 2005.

Each project is funded for a period of up to three years. The maximum total Federal award for the entire three year period is $800,000 per project. Grantees are required to make a non-financial or cash recipient contribution (match) of five percent of the total grant award.

States may use funds awarded through the ADRC grants program to better coordinate and/or redesign their existing systems of information, assistance, and access. ADRC functions are performed in a single location in some communities. Other communities decentralize ADRC functions. In the latter case, ADRCs may have multiple sites and organizations involved in performing the information and access functions. Some communities have different access points for different populations.

Examples of ADRCs in Action

Alaska

ADRC Name	ADRC Website	Lead Agency	Project Period
Alaska Aging & Disability Resource Center	*Pending*	Alaska Housing & Finance Corporation	2004 Grantee

Alaska will establish five regional ADRCs operated by the State Centers for Independent Living (SILC) to provide citizen-centered "one-stop shopping" entry to long-term support services for seniors and people with disabilities statewide. The ADRCs will offer information and referral services, eligibility screening, assistance in gaining access to long-term support services for private pay consumers, comprehensive assessment for those seeking publicly funded services, programmatic eligibility determination for long-term support services, and access to the Division of Public Assistance for Medicaid financial eligibility determination. The SILC will work with the Division of Senior and Disability Services and the Senior Housing Office to develop a management information system that tracks consumer intake, needs assessment, care plans, utilization, and costs. Formative and summative evaluations will be conducted by the Center for Human Development.

Florida

ADRC Name	ADRC Website	Lead Agency	Project Period
Florida Aging and Disability Resource Center	*Pending*	Florida Department of Elder Affairs (DOEA)	2004 Grantee

Florida will develop and implement ADRCs operated by area agencies on aging in at least two Planning and Service Areas (PSAs) for both publicly and privately funded services for the elderly and individuals with mental illness. Florida will co-locate Information and Referral, screening and assessment, access to crisis intervention, medical and financial eligibility determination, and long-term services and supports counseling. It will establish a single administrative structure accessible through multiple locations (senior centers, Area Administration on Aging, housing authorities, mental health centers, etc.) in each of the ADRC communities. Access to ADRC services will also be available by phone and the Internet. The ADRC program will benefit from a current state project designed to merge existing program information and management databases. Since the announcement of the 2004 ADRC grant, the Florida Legislature passed statutory changes to implement Aging Resource Centers (ARCs) statewide for the aging population only. Only adults 60 and older will be targeted for service in the ADRC's first year. Adults 60 and older and adults 18 and older with severe mental illness are targeted for service in the ADRC's second and third years.

Wisconsin

ADRC Name	ADRC Website	Lead Agency	Project Period
Lessons Learned: Redefining the Expansion of Wisconsin Resource Centers	Pending	Wisconsin Department of Health and Family Services (DHFS)	2004 Grantee

The Wisconsin DHFS will expand geographic coverage of their full-service Aging and Disability Resource Centers, develop capacity for all target groups to be served, and develop an infrastructure to support ultimate expansion to all parts of the state. Five local agencies will be selected through an RFP process to develop new full-service ADRCs. DHFS will develop state-level infrastructure to support current and future development of a statewide system of full-service ADRCs that serve elders and at least one other target population of individuals with disabilities and have a strong collaboration with local programs. The state infrastructure will include:

- Two toolkits, one to promote public awareness and one for long-term services and supports options counseling;
- Identification of information management system solutions to meet state and local needs for consistent data collection and reporting;
- Ability to provide technical assistance in adding new target populations, including people with mental illness; and
- Technical assistance in identifying and accessing funding sources and in accessing services already available.

Looking Forward

AoA and CMS will evaluate whether the ADRCs increase informed decisionmaking and consumer satisfaction with access to needed long-term supports and services in the most integrated setting. Over a three-year period, each of the pilot states is expected to have at least one operating center that demonstrates improvements in the state's ability to manage public resources, monitor program quality and costs, and improve assessment of need and effective coordination of services to limit unnecessary use of high cost options, including nursing facilities.

Additional Resources for More Information

Aging and Disability Resource Centers, Background Information on ADRCs, *available at:* http://www.aoa.gov/prof/aging_dis/background.asp .

Centers for Medicare and Medicaid Services New Freedom Initiative website, *available at:* http://www.cms.hhs.gov/newfreedom .

ADRC Technical Assistance Exchange website, *available at:* http://www.adrc-tae.org.

Questions and Answers about the Aging and Disability Resource Center Grants Program, created by the Administration on Aging and Centers for Medicare & Medicaid Services, *available at:* http://www.aoa.gov/prof/aging_dis/AoACMSQA%20071403.pdf .

Fact Sheet on the Aging and Disability Resource Centers, created by the U.S. Department of Health and Human Services, Administration on Aging, *available at:* http://www.aoa.gov/press/fact/pdf/fs_aging_disability.pdf.

CONSOLIDATING ACCESS TO INFORMATION AND SERVICES: LEARNING FROM THE STATES

The AdvantAge Initiative 2003 National Survey of Adults Aged 65 and Older[1] asked respondents across the country many questions about their physical and mental health, their knowledge about and use of services in their communities, their physical and social activities, and aspects of their communities that make them "livable" for older people, as well as areas that need improvement. One of the questions they were asked was, "What is the best resource, such as a person or an organization, in your city, town, or county to get information on various services," and in response, fully 20 percent, or one in five, older people said "I don't know." This 20 percent represents 6.7 million Americans aged 65 and older who don't know where to turn when they need information and services.

There are almost 900,000 non-profit organizations in the U.S. plus scores of government agencies that provide services. People looking for assistance have trouble navigating this complicated web of health and human service programs; often people don't even know where to begin. To help remedy this situation, in recent years states across the U.S. have been making progress toward consolidating disparate information and referral services using an easy-to-remember three-digit dialing telephone code reserved by the Federal Communications Commission (FCC) for this purpose.

Background: The 2-1-1 Information and Referral System

Community Information and Referral, often referred to simply as I&R, has been a staple of the health and human services industry for the past 50 years. Comprehensive and specialized I&R agencies provide linkages between individuals and the often daunting maze of services available in their communities. I&R services help people living in the community negotiate this maze by maintaining comprehensive databases of resources and making them available by telephone, the internet, and through paper directories or handbooks. I&R specialists are trained professionals who work with callers to find the help they need. They assess callers' needs and help them determine their options and best courses of action. I&R specialists also are trained to intervene in crisis situations, determine whether a caller is eligible for programs, and advocate on behalf of the caller.

In the past, most I&R telephone help lines have been 10-digit local telephone numbers or toll-free numbers serving a circumscribed area. But on July 21, 2000, the Federal Communications Commission assigned the dialing code 2-1-1 to be used exclusively for community information and referral purposes, and in many communities this central phone number has replaced individual agency help lines as the source of choice for residents seeking information and referral.

While the specific services offered through 2-1-1, as well as the degree of accessibility of 2-1-1's telephone and website services for people with disabilities, vary from community to community, in general 2-1-1 offers information about and referral to the following types of services:

- Basic human needs resources: food banks, clothing, shelters, rent assistance, utility assistance
- Physical and mental health resources: medical information lines, crisis intervention services, support groups, counseling, drug and alcohol intervention, rehabilitation, health insurance programs, Medicaid and Medicare, maternal health, children's health insurance
- Employment support: unemployment benefits, financial assistance, job training, transportation assistance, education programs
- Support for older Americans and persons with disabilities: home health care, adult day care, congregate meals, Meals on Wheels, respite care, transportation, and homemaker services
- Support for children, youth, and families: quality childcare, Success by Six, after school programs, Head Start, family resource centers,

summer camps and recreation programs, mentoring, tutoring, protective services

- Volunteer opportunities and donations[2]

2-1-1 in the States

The 2-1-1 help line was first launched by the United Way of Metropolitan Atlanta in 1997—several years before the FCC made the number universal. United Way chapters around the country have a long tradition of funding I&R services in their respective communities and since 1997 have continued to be involved in starting up and supporting 2-1-1 services in states around the country.

There are now 157 active 2-1-1 systems covering all or part of 32 states, Washington, D.C., and Puerto Rico and serving 40 percent of the U.S. population. In some parts of the country 2-1-1 is a well-known and well-used resource. Puerto Rico and 13 states have implemented 2-1-1 statewide,[3] so that residents across each of these states have access to 2-1-1 information systems. In many other parts of the country, however, 2-1-1 is just in the planning stages. Many, but not all, of the existing 2-1-1 lines in the states that have them are available 24 hours per day, 7 days per week. Some locales have made their databases available on the internet so that people may access information at times of the day when 2-1-1 is not available.

Connecticut was the first state in the country to implement 2-1-1 statewide. The number—called 2-1-1 Infoline—went into effect in March 1999, replacing a toll-free number. Infoline can be accessed from anywhere in Connecticut. Help is available 24 hours a day, every day of the year. Infoline has multilingual caseworkers and is accessible by TTY to people who are deaf or hard of hearing. Infoline has developed the most comprehensive database of human service resources in the state of Connecticut. The database is continually updated and is also available on CD-ROM and the Internet.[4] Caller demographics and problems collected by 2-1-1 provide valuable information to state agencies, which use the information to understand the overall problems facing Connecticut residents and assess needs in the state. Since Connecticut switched to 2-1-1 from a 10-digit, toll-free number, the volume of calls increased from 200,000 in 1999 to over 320,000 in 2003. Top service requests were for utilities/heat, housing, mental health services, financial assistance, and health care.[5] Not all the statewide 2-1-1 information lines are as well developed as Connecticut's, largely due to lack of sufficient funding and legislative support.

Aloha United Way was launched in Hawaii in July 2002, making Hawaii the second state in the nation with statewide 2-1-1 service. People can call 2-1-1 from all islands 24 hours a day, 7 days a week for information on more than 4,000 government and non-profit programs and services. New Jersey's statewide 2-1-1 service came on line in February, 2005 and is available to all New Jersey residents, including cell phone users.[6] The Idaho 211 project is using AmeriCorps and AmeriCorps VISTA Volunteers to identify community resources through community asset mapping activities, and this information will be integrated into Idaho CareLine's (Idaho's official 2-1-1 call center) databases. Vermont's collaborative partners in their statewide 2-1-1 line include the Vermont Agency of Human Services, area agencies on aging, Vermont Department of Libraries, Vermont E-911, Vermont Emergency Management, Vermont Network Against Domestic and Sexual Violence, and information and referral/assistance providers statewide. In Texas, the State Legislature is encouraging all state agencies to coordinate their I&R services with Texas's statewide 2-1-1. For information about the status of other state 2-1-1 efforts, see www.211.org.

Funding and Cost-Savings

The 2-1-1 call centers are generally supported through a combination of funding sources, including local United Way chapters, community foundations, and federal and local governments. However, this patchwork of funding is often insufficient to start up or maintain full-service 2-1-1 call centers.

Senators Elizabeth Dole (R-NC), Hillary Rodham Clinton (D-NY), and Richard Burr (R-NC) and Representatives Michael Bilirakis (R-FL9) and Anna Eshoo (D-CA14) have introduced the Calling for 2-1-1 Act that would authorize $150 million for two years, and $100 million for the next three years, in federal funds to assist states with implementing and sustaining 2-1-1 statewide. This federal investment would need to be leveraged in states with a minimum of 50 percent of program funding from state and local government and private sources such as corporate, foundation, and United Way dollars. The rationale behind this cost-sharing is that 2-1-1 is most effective when built on solid public/private partnerships and with a diverse and sustainable funding base. The Act closed the 108th Congress with 182 bi-partisan congressional sponsors.

A national cost benefit analysis conducted by the University of Texas estimates a net value to society of a national 2-1-1 system approaching $130 million in the first year alone and a conservative estimate of $1.1 billion over ten years. Savings include time saved, tax assistance and recovery, volunteer recruitment, around the clock service, a reduction in the number of 1-800 numbers, and a reduction in non-emergency calls to 9-1-1.[7]

Resources

As the first state to implement 2-1-1, Connecticut helps other regions develop their own 2-1-1 call centers (see www.infoline.org for more information)

www.211.org and www.airs.org are comprehensive websites that provide a variety of information about 2-1-1 and tools for starting up and maintaining 2-1-1 lines

End Notes

[1] Center for Home Care Policy and Research, Visiting Nurse Service of N.Y. (2004) The AdvantAge Initiative National Survey of Adults Aged 65 and Older. Available at: www.advantageinitiative.org
[2] www.211.org
[3] Vermont, Massachusetts, New Jersey, West Virginia, Louisiana, Texas, Iowa, Wisconsin, Minnesota, North Dakota, Vermont, Idaho, and Hawaii.
[4] www.infoline.org
[5] www.211.org
[6] Many 211 lines do not accept calls from cell phones
[7] Ibid.

In: Creating Livable Communities for People... ISBN: 978-1-60741-534-3
Editor: Alise Vanags

Chapter 3

STRATEGY TWO: UTILIZATION OF FAVORABLE TAX TREATMENT (E.G. TAX CREDITS) TO STIMULATE CHANGE IN INDIVIDUAL AND CORPORATE BEHAVIOR THAT ENCOURAGES INVESTMENT IN LIVABLE COMMUNITY OBJECTIVES

National Council on Disability

The availability of appropriate and affordable housing choices is one of the most important measures of community livability. As the examples below illustrate, Strategy Two can be used to expand such housing opportunities for people with low incomes and/or people with disabilities and ensure that the housing is affordable and accessible.

LOW INCOME HOUSING TAX CREDITS

Housing is a cornerstone of livable communities and the demand for affordable, accessible housing for people with disabilities has not gone unaddressed by the Federal Government. As part of the Tax Reform Act of 1986, the Federal Government created the Low Income Housing Tax Credit

(LIHTC) to encourage the production and redevelopment of livable, affordable rental housing across the nation.

The Low Income Housing Tax Credit is a way for states to encourage private investment in sustainable, livable communities for people with disabilities without having to allocate direct federal expenditures. The LIHTC is a significant source of financing for developers seeking to construct and rehabilitate housing opportunities for people with disabilities.

Virtually all people with disabilities receiving Supplemental Security Income (SSI) are theoretically eligible for the affordable housing units in LIHTC properties because they have incomes far below 50 percent or 60 percent of area median income. On average, the national income of a person receiving SSI is equal to 18 percent of area median income.[1] However, the problem for many people with disabilities is that, given their income, the tax credit rents for the affordable units in LIHTC properties are too high. In certain localities with relatively low tax credit rents, *if* two people with disabilities are willing to share a unit, or if both members of a two-person household receive SSI, the tax credit rent may be affordable. But in many localities, the tax credit rent charged in a LIHTC property may be higher than a person's entire SSI monthly income.[2]

Why should the disability community care about this complicated program if it doesn't provide units that are affordable to people with disabilities receiving SSI? There are at least three reasons:[3]

1. The owners of LIHTC-financed properties are *required* to accept Section 8 vouchers.
2. States are increasingly using LIHTC in combination with an array of other affordable housing resources in order to achieve what is called "deeper income targeting," which means that they are trying to serve people with much lower incomes than 50 percent or 60 percent of area median income.
3. The LIHTC program is being used more and more to create permanent supportive housing for people with disabilities, including chronically homeless people with disabilities.

Program Background

Under the LIHTC program, states are authorized to issue federal tax credits for the acquisition, rehabilitation, or new construction of affordable rental housing. The credits can be used by property owners to offset taxes on other income, and are generally sold to outside investors to raise initial development funds for a project.

To qualify for credits, a project must have a specific proportion of its units set aside for lower income households. Rents and utilities in these units, which are classified as general household expenses, are limited to 30 percent of the qualifying income. The amount of the credit that can be provided for a project is a function of development cost (excluding land), the proportion of units set aside, and the credit rate (which varies based on development method and whether other federal subsidies are used). Credits provide equity into a project, and they are provided for a period of 10 years.

As of 2004, the LIHTC program generated $6 billion in housing investments and created more than 115,000 affordable rental housing units nationwide each year for low-income families, seniors, the homeless, and people with disabilities. The program's structure allows developers to raise equity through partnerships with tax credit investors, leverage private and public funds, and secure additional funding to cover construction and permanent costs. These costs include loans and grants to create, for example, child care facilities and accessible community rooms.

The Federal Government allocates to each state a certain number of budgeted LIHTCs that are issued by each state's housing agency to developers of qualified low-income housing. The credits are allocated based upon the cost of property, less land and non-eligible expenses. The property generates tax credits once construction is completed and the property is occupied by the required number of qualified tenants. So long as the property remains in use to rent to qualified tenants for the requisite period of time, that property will generate a steady flow of tax credits for ten consecutive years.

Program Description

The Internal Revenue Service (IRS) oversees LIHTC compliance to ensure that states and investors do not use more tax credits than authorized. The U.S. Department of Housing and Urban Development (HUD), though not formally responsible for program oversight, monitors and analyzes the tax credits because of the program's important role in providing for the housing needs of low-income people.

Program Overview

Each state receives an allocation of LIHTCs on a per capita basis. In 2004, the limit was $1.80 multiplied by the state's population, with a minimum of $2,075,000 per state. The credits are competitively awarded under Section 42 of the Internal Revenue Code and the state's Qualified Allocation Plan.

Developers who receive tax credits may syndicate (sell) the credits to raise equity (cash) for development. In exchange for receiving long-term income in the form of an allotment of LIHTCs, the developer agrees to comply with pre-determined rent restrictions. Each dollar of LIHTC allocated entitles the syndicator to one dollar of credit against their corporate income tax every year for ten years.

State housing agencies put each development through three separate, rigorous financial evaluations to make sure the development receives only enough credits to make it viable as long-term, low-income housing. Only investors in properties that pass all three reviews, complete their developments, and actually rent them to low-income families can claim the credits.

At a minimum, either 20 percent or more of the units in a given development must be occupied by individuals whose incomes are below 50 percent of the area median income, or at least 40 percent of the units must be occupied by individuals below 60 percent of the area median income. LIHTC financed units must remain affordable to low-income people for at least 30 years, and many are permanently dedicated to low-income use.

On average, LIHTCs generate over 40 percent of development costs. Remaining financing typically comes from market-rate first mortgages and low or no-interest second mortgages, often from HOME or other public sources.

Calculating the Credit

The credit is based upon prevailing Treasury interest rates. The "9% Projects" credit is calculated so that the present value of the annual credits over the 10-year period equals 70 percent of the building costs. The "4% Projects" credit is available for new construction and substantial rehabilitation projects. 4% Projects are often awarded to projects that utilize mortgage revenue bond financing, also known as non-competitive credits. A developer cannot use both 4% and 9% credits. A project must use one or the other, or the LIHTC can be combined with Historical Rehabilitation Credits and New Markets Tax Credits.

Applying the Credit

The LIHTCs that may be claimed are calculated by multiplying the applicable credit percentage by the building's "qualified basis." The first step in making this calculation is determining a building's "eligible basis," i.e. the cost for the entire building, including non-low-income units if the quality of those units is comparable to that of the low-income units. The eligible basis is determined at the end of the first year of the credit period (subject to reduction for federal subsidies). Only building costs are included, not land costs.

For acquisitions, only depreciable property is included in the basis. Projects involving substantial rehabilitation may include only expenditures within a 24-month period that can be capitalized. "Substantial rehabilitation" means that rehabilitation expenses either must equal at least 10 percent of the building's adjusted basis at the beginning of the 24-month period or cost at least $3,000 per unit, whichever is greater. For new construction, only costs that can be capitalized are included. Also, the eligible basis may be increased to 130 percent for new construction in areas of difficult development or high-cost adjustment.

The building's qualified basis is then calculated as the portion of the eligible basis that is used for low-income tenants, based on the percentage of total units or floor space, whichever is less. The initial qualified basis is determined on the last day of the first year the building is placed in service or, at the owner's election, on the last day of the following year. The owner must maintain the initial qualified basis throughout the 15-year compliance period.

Syndicating the Credit

Developers and sponsors of projects that win the 9% Project credits through the competitive process will sell or syndicate the credits to individuals and companies who invest cash into the project in exchange for the tax credits. The credits can be sold and structured as an equity fund, generally financing multiple projects. Alternatively, the credits can be sold directly to individual investors or corporations, generally on a project-specific basis. The money raised by the sale of the tax credits is project equity, thereby reducing the financing needs and costs of the project, with the resulting cost savings going to the residents.

Developers sell to investors the right to take these credits over ten years. The price paid for the credits reflects the value of the real estate, quality of development, and net present value of the 10 years worth of credits. Tax credits are sold on the basis of their present value, so are discounted to 75–80 cents on the dollar. For example, $1 million in tax credits would generate about $750,000 to $850,000 in equity for the project developer. Maryland's $10.5 million allocation of LIHTC, for example, raises $80 to $90 million in private money for affordable housing annually.

Generally, the sale of the credits is accomplished through a third party syndicator who sells the credits to companies or individuals in need of tax relief (i.e. the investors). The investors then form a limited partnership with ownership interest in the project, while the sponsor (developer) is the general partner with responsibility for project management, construction, and compliance to tax credit restrictions. As an alternative, an investor may purchase credits in a pool or fund, and the revenues generated will provide equity for a number of different projects. Syndicators establish discrete funds as investment opportunities, with responsibilities for selling the credits, evaluating eligible projects and making awards, and assisting through the construction and compliance stages of the project. Each investor enjoys a pro-rata share of the credits consistent with its percentage of ownership in the pool.

The Role of States in Shaping Rental Housing Policy for Persons with Disabilities

Each state receives an annual "budget" of tax credit authority that can be used to reduce the federal tax liability of investors in affordable rental developments. The state passes on this tax credit authority to individual developments, based on a Qualified Allocation Plan (QAP). The QAP establishes criteria for the annual selection of developments around the state that will be built or preserved using LIHTC.

Through the QAP and review of individual proposals for housing developments, state policy-makers shape the way in which affordable rental housing is distributed geographically and to different types of families and individuals, including persons with disabilities. The QAP is developed through a consultative process that also gives advocates at the state level an opportunity to affect housing policy.

QAPs vary widely from state to state over time. Many states hold competitions based on set-asides of the tax credit to specific metropolitan and non-metropolitan areas within the state, while most others establish preferences for specific types of geographic areas. Sometimes sub-allocation follows population types and needs, while sometimes areas are believed to have greater relative need for affordable housing and, as a result, are favored. The state QAP has a base-line point value that developers must meet in order to be considered. States award additional points to applications based on state priorities.

The success of a developer's proposal to use LIHTCs allocated through a QAP can be greatly affected by a small number of points at the margin when all applications are similar for low-income rental developments. States tend to allot between 1.5 and 3 percent of the available points in a QAP to proposed developments that specifically provide affordable, accessible housing to people with disabilities. Thus, developers who develop this kind of housing will receive an additional allotment of credits. State LIHTC allocations tend to emphasize developing geographic areas that have both needy households and shortages of rental housing.

Resources Used

The LIHTC program has recently been amended to give States the equivalent of nearly $5 billion in annual budget authority to issue tax credits. As a housing-related tax expenditure, the LIHTC does not require direct appropriations. The estimated cost to the federal treasury in FY 2003 was $6.2 billion.

In 2000, Congress increased the LIHTC annual cap by 40 percent to restore purchasing power lost to inflation since Congress imposed the cap in 1986 and indexed the cap to inflation beginning in 2003. The 2004 limit is $1.80 multiplied by state population, with a minimum of $2,075,000 per state.

When the LIHTC program was made permanent in 1993, corporations began acquiring the credits directly and through syndication funds. Corporations now constitute virtually the entire market of LIHTC investors and include banks and insurance companies as well as Fannie Mae and Freddie Mac.

In 2004, States allocated over $504 million in tax credits and allocated over $533 million in 2005. The allocation of credits ranged from just under $2 million worth of credits in Delaware to $50 million in credits in California.

It is clear that through the QAP or through the selection of individual LIHTC developments, state policymakers are making critical choices about rental housing policy that affects the well-being of individual households and the economic health of the state's metropolitan areas. These choices will help create public-private investments and partnerships and accelerate the development of sustainable, livable communities for people with disabilities and their families.

State housing planners are in a particularly good position to design housing options for people with disabilities, since other support systems for the same populations are funded and regulated at the state level. Through both QAPs and the selection of individual LIHTC developments, state housing program administrators can encourage the development of housing that fills gaps in the current system of housing alternatives, including alternatives to rental housing funded by the federal Section 811 program.

States that ensure point allotments through subcategorizing "Housing for People with Disabilities" in their QAP "Special Needs Housing" category are in the best position to ensure that LIHTCs will be used by developers to construct affordable, accessible, and integrated housing for people with disabilities.

State Examples

Iowa

The State of Iowa is an example of how a state can use the tax credits program to achieve a policy of expanding affordable, accessible housing opportunities for people with disabilities.

The Iowa Finance Authority (IFA, www.ifahome.com) oversees Iowa's distribution of LIHTCs. IFA established that 30 percent of all the LIHTCs issued by IFA are used as equity investments in affordable, accessible, and integrated housing developments.

To qualify for this set-aside: (1) 25 to 49 percent of the units in the proposed project must be set aside for people with disabilities within an integrated setting or a setting that promotes homeownership, or (2) 50 to 100 percent of the units must be set-aside for people with disabilities within a single-purpose setting. Any unused tax credits remaining from the set-aside are returned to the general pool and allocated in the current year. To receive an allocation of the credits, a developer must submit a supportive services plan in addition to the application.

IFA allocates tax credits from this 30 percent set-aside based upon the QAP. Service-enriched housing projects are scored with all the projects except that the 30 percent set-aside is available in its entirety until the set-aside is fully allocated. If the set-aside is exhausted, projects proposed for the service-enriched housing set-aside are permitted to compete in the set-asides for which the project is eligible.

In addition to the set-aside for projects that create accessible, affordable, and integrated housing, IFA has taken another substantial step to aid in the construction or rehabilitation of housing for people with disabilities. Under

IFA's current project scoring criteria, projects designed to serve a special needs population receive 30 points out of a possible 325 points, or 9.2 percent of the available points, as opposed to the usual 5 to 10 points, or between 1.5 and 3 percent of available points, in the majority of states.

In 2005, Iowa financed 19 projects for a total of $40,159,320 in credits. Two hundred and eleven of the 533 units constructed with LIHTCs in Iowa are for people with disabilities. Seven of the 19 funded projects are for service-enriched housing, which will provide new and preserve existing housing opportunities for people with disabilities.

Maryland

The State of Maryland is another example of how states are allotting their LIHTCs. The Maryland Department of Housing and Community Development (www2.dhcd.state.md.us/Website/home/index.aspx) oversees Maryland's distribution of tax credits.

Unlike Iowa, Maryland does not have a set-aside for projects that construct or rehabilitate affordable, accessible housing for people with disabilities. Maryland's legislature recognizes that people with disabilities are historically "isolate[d], and ... such forms of discrimination against individuals with disabilities [will] continue to be a serious and pervasive social problem." Like many other states that recognize this need, Maryland has not yet fully leveraged their LIHTCs as a means to accelerate the development of housing for people with disabilities.

Current statistics indicate that nearly 157,000 residents of Maryland will have a need for some form of affordable, low-income housing over the next ten years. Statistics further indicate that, over the next ten years, approximately 29,000 residents with disabilities in Maryland will need some form of affordable, accessible housing.

Maryland's QAP makes "Housing for Disabled or Other Special Needs Linked to Supportive Services" a single category. Maryland awards a maximum of 10 points, 1.5 percent of the total available points, for "Housing for Disabled or Other Special Needs."

In 2004, Maryland allotted nearly $10 million in tax credits. Sixty-seven of the units that received LIHTCs are accessible for people with disabilities. Thirty-seven of those 67 units are only available to elderly Marylanders. In 2003, Maryland awarded LIHTCs to 26 projects with 207 units considered accessible for people with disabilities. Seventy-four of those accessible units are only available to elderly Marylanders. Maryland is moving forward to explore new ways to use LIHTCs to accelerate the development of appropriate housing for these populations.

Additional Opportunities: The Homeownership Tax Credit

Proposed in mid-March of 2005, the Homeownership Tax Credit (HOTC) would increase housing opportunities for working families by helping to bridge the gap between what it costs to build homes in lower-income neighborhoods and the price that buyers in those neighborhoods can afford to pay.[4] The HOTC is another lever through which public-private investments can be created that accelerate the development of sustainable livable communities.

The HOTC is generally targeted to census tracts with median incomes of 80 percent or less of the area or state median income. Areas eligible under federal rural housing programs and Native American areas are eligible as well. States are able to use a portion of their credit authority in other economically distressed areas. Eligible buyers generally are those whose incomes do not exceed 80 percent of area median income. In certain distressed neighborhoods, eligible buyers can earn up to 100 percent of the greater of area median income.

The program is structured in such a way that states will receive annual allocations of credit authority starting at $1.75 per capita and rising with inflation. States will award credits to developers under a competitive process in accordance with annual plans for meeting state home ownership needs. Developers that receive credit allocations will be allowed to sell them to investors and use the proceeds to bridge the gap between the development costs and the sales price of homes they develop. The credit will cover up to 50 percent of acquisition and development costs for either new construction or substantial rehabilitation.

The HOTC will help produce roughly 250,000 new homes, almost all for low-income people, over a five year period, at a federal cost of just over $2.5 billion. This activity will help generate more than half a million jobs, $20 billion in wages, and $10 billion in federal, state, and local revenue. The development and economic activity that the HOTC will generate will also help close minority and low-income homeownership gaps and stabilize struggling neighborhoods.

Resources

United States Department of Housing and Urban Development

Office of Policy Development and Research. http://www.huduser.org .

Low income Housing Tax Credits Data Sets. Available at: http://www.huduser.org/datasets/lihtc.html .

United States Department of Housing and Urban Development, Office of Policy Development and Research, *Updating the Low income Housing Tax Credit Database: Projects Placed in Service Through 2001.* available at: http://www.huduser.org/Datasets/lihtc/report9501.pdf .

Fair Housing and Equal Opportunity Office. http://www.hud.gov/offices/fheo/index.cfm .

Memorandum of Understanding Among the Department of the Treasury, The Department of Housing and Urban Development, and The Department of Justice. Available at: http://www.hud.gov/offices/fheo/lihtcmou.cfm .

Office of Community Planning and Development. http://www.hud.gov/offices/cpd/index.cfm.

HOME and Low Income Housing Tax Credits, available at: http://www.hud.gov/offices/cpd/affordablehousing/training/lihtc/index.cfm

LIHTC Basics, available at: http://www.hud.gov/offices/cpd/affordablehousing/training/lihtc/basics/index.cfm .

How do Housing Tax Credits Work?, available at: http://www.hud.gov/offices/cpd/affordablehousing/training/lihtc/basics/work.cfm .

Allocating Housing Tax Credits, available at: http://www.hud.gov/offices/cpd/affordablehousing/training/lihtc/basics/allocating.cfm .

Eligibility, available at: http://www.hud.gov/offices/cpd/affordable housing/training/lihtc/basics/eligibility.cfm

Syndication, available at: http://www.hud.gov/offices/cpd/affordable housing/training/lihtc/basics/syndication.cfm .

Other Resources

Websites

1. The Affordable Housing Resource Center, http://www.novoco.com/resource.shtml.

Articles

1. National Council on Disability, Reconstructing Fair Housing, *available at:* http://www.ncd.gov/newsroom/publications/2001/pdf/fairhousing.pdf#search= 'reconstructing%20fair%20housing' (last viewed February 21, 2005).
2. Denise DiPasquale and Matthew E. Kahn, *Measuring Neighborhood Investments: An Examination of Community Choice*, 27 Real Estate Economics 389 (1999), *available at*: http://www.cityresearch.com/pubs/Measuring%20Neighborhood%20Investments1.pdf (last viewed January 13, 2005).
3. Denise DiPasquale, et. al, *Comparing the Costs of Federal Housing Assistance Programs*, FRBNY Economic Policy Review 147 (June 2003), *available at:*http://www.cityresearch.com/pubs/NY%20Fed%20Cost%20Paper.pdf (last viewed January 13, 2005).
4. Jean Cummings and Denise DiPasquale, *Building Affordable Rental Housing*, February 1998, *available at*: http://www.cityresearch.com/lihtc/cr_lihtc.pdf (last viewed January 13, 2005).
5. Jean Cummings and Denise DiPasquale, *The Low income Housing Tax Credit: An Analysis of the First Ten Years*, 10 Housing Policy Debate 251, *available at*: http://www.cityresearch.com/pubs/cummings.pdf (last viewed January 13, 2005).
6. Alan Mallach, *Toward a Policy Framework for the Allocation of Low income Housing Tax Credits*, *available at:* http://www.njisj.org/reports/framework_report.html . (last viewed February 21, 2005).

State Housing Agencies

Alabama	http://www.ahfa. com/	Alaska	http://www.ahfc.state.ak.us/
Arizona	http://www.housingaz.com/	Arkansas	http://www.arkansas.gov/adfa/
California	http://www.hcd.ca.gov/	Colorado	http://www.dola.state.co.us/doh/Index.htm
Connecticut	http://www.chfa.org/MainPages/default.asp	Delaware	http://www2.state.de.us/dsha/
District of Columbia	http://dhcd.dc.gov	Florida	http://www.floridahousing.org/
Georgia	http://www.dca.state.ga.us/	Hawaii	http://www.hawaii.gov/portal/
Idaho	http://www.ihfa.org/	Illinois	http://www.ihda.org/
Indiana	http://www.state.in.us/ihfa/	Iowa	http://www.ifahome.com/
Kansas	http://www.kshousingcorp.org/	Kentucky	http://www.kyhousing.org/
Louisiana	http://www.lhfa.state.la.us/	Maine	http://www.mainehousing.org/
Maryland	http://www.dhcd.state.md.us/	Massachusetts	http://www.mass.gov/dhcd/
Michigan	http://www.michigan.gov/mshda	Minnesota	http://www.mhfa.state.mn.us/
Mississippi	http://www.mshomecorp.com/firstpage.htm	Missouri	http://www.mhdc.com/
Montana	http://housing.state.mt.us/	Nebraska	http://www.nifa.org/
Nevada	http://nvhousing.state.nv.us/	New Hampshire	http://www.nhhfa.org/
New Jersey	http://www.state.nj.us/dca/hmfa/	New Mexico	http://www.nmmfa.org/
New York	http://www.dhcr.state.ny.us/ocd/progs/lihc/ ocdli0.htm and http://www.nyhomes.org/default.htm	North Carolina	http://www.nchfa.com/
North Dakota	http://www.ndhfa.state.nd.us/	Ohio	http://www.odod.state.oh.us/ohfa/
Oklahoma	http://www.ohfa.org//	Oregon	http://www.ohcs.oregon.gov/
Pennsylvania	http://www.phfa.org/	Rhode Island	http://www.rihousing.com/
South Carolina	http://www.sha.state.sc.us/	South Dakota	http://www.sdhda.org/
Tennessee	http://www.state.tn.us/thda/	Texas	http://www.tdhca.state.tx.us/
Utah	http://www.utahhousingcorp.org/	Vermont	http://www.vhfa.org/
Virginia	http://www.vhda.com/vhda_com/front_page/default.asp	Washington	http://www.wshfc.org/
West Virginia	http://www.wvhdf.com/	Wisconsin	http://www.wheda.com/
Wyoming	http://www.wyomingcda.com/		

Expanding the Supply of Affordable, Accessible Housing: Learning from Kentucky

As the description of low income housing tax credits demonstrates, "financial carrots" are effective in stimulating the development of affordable housing. Incentives can also be used to encourage the adoption of universal design principles in the building of affordable housing. In Kentucky, builders and developers whose rental housing and/or single family home construction or rehabilitation projects are partially (50%) or wholly financed by the Kentucky Housing Corporation (KHC), *must* follow KHC's Universal Design Policy. This policy, in effect since 1993, is designed to "ensure that much of the housing produced with KHC financing meets the needs of the greatest number of people for the longest period of time."

Background

The Kentucky Housing Corporation (KHC) is Kentucky's state housing finance agency. It was created in 1972 by the state's General Assembly and is a self-supporting public corporation of the Commonwealth of Kentucky, administratively attached to the Finance and Administration Cabinet.[5] A portion of KHC funds is derived from the interest earned through the sale of tax-exempt mortgage revenue bonds, which has enabled thousands of low and moderate-income Kentucky families to find and live in affordable homes. KHC also receives fees for administering federal housing programs that make affordable housing available to low-income families.

KHC administers and monitors a number of federal and state affordable housing programs, such as:

- The HOME Program, a federal program that provides funding for various types of affordable housing production and rehabilitation (KHC also assists with the state matching funds requirement in the HOME Program)
- The Affordable Housing Trust Fund, a state program that supports the acquisition, rehabilitation, and new construction of very low-income housing units and provides matching funds for federal housing programs requiring a state or local match

- The Small Multifamily Affordable Loan Program (SMAL), a state program designed to increase the supply of affordable rental housing for lower-income individuals, particularly in rural areas of the state
- The Housing Development Fund, a state program that provides flexible, low-interest rate construction loans for new construction, rehabilitation, site or land development, acquisition, or construction of prototype affordable housing
- A number of other financing mechanisms that are designed to increase affordable and accessible housing stock in the state, including a new program called the Permanent Supportive Housing Initiative that provides non-profit and for-profit housing developers a zero percent revolving loan fund to cover predevelopment costs as well as grants to fund supportive services.[6]

In 1996, the Kentucky General Assembly established a state policy on housing. The Commonwealth of Kentucky Housing Policy Act sets a number of objectives, including the following:

- Identify the basic housing needs of all Kentuckians, including the elderly, persons of low and very low-income, the disabled, the homeless, and single-parent households
- Coordinate housing activities and services among state departments and agencies to ensure program flexibility and comprehensive housing production
- Remove administrative and regulatory guidelines to ensure compatibility in the development of affordable housing for all Kentuckians
- Encourage and strengthen collaborative planning and partnerships among social service providers, all levels of government, and the public and private sectors, including for-profit and non-profit organizations, in the production of affordable housing[7]

In 2001, Kentucky became one of the first states to receive a Real Choice Systems Change Grant for Community Living from the Centers for Medicare and Medicaid Services (CMS), the federal agency that administers the Medicare and Medicaid programs. The purpose of the grant program is to build infrastructure that will result in effective and enduring improvements in community long-term service and support systems. These systemic changes are designed to enable children and adults of any age who have a disability or long-term illness to:

- Live in the most integrated community setting appropriate to their individual support requirements and preferences
- Exercise meaningful choices about their living environment, the providers of services they receive, the types of supports they use and the manner by which services are provided
- Obtain quality services in a manner as consistent as possible with their community living preferences and priorities.[8]

Two of the long-term services and supports system problems Kentucky identified in its Real Choice grant application were related to housing:

- Lack of funding for transition programs and limited housing options to allow individuals to live in community-integrated settings
- Lack of communication among local public housing agencies, service providers, and advocates about the housing needs of people with disabilities

To remedy this situation, Kentucky proposed to increase the stock of new, affordable, and accessible housing options, facilitate transitions to community living for people with disabilities and, "through partnerships with state and local housing agencies, ensure that new housing is fully accessible and incorporates universal design principles."[9]

Developing Universal Design Principles

With support from the CMS Real Choice grant and input from the public through public hearings and partners across the state, the Department of Design and Construction Review of the Kentucky Housing Corporation developed a *Universal Design Handbook*[10] for use by builders and developers in the construction and reconstruction of affordable housing. The Universal Design Policy went into effect on January 1, 2003.

While housing that incorporates universal design can clearly benefit people with disabilities, the Department of Design and Construction Review's definition of universal design does not target any group in particular. In fact, their definition is all-inclusive and stresses the wide-ranging and lifelong benefits of housing built according to universal design principles:

"Universal design is a building concept that incorporates products, general design layouts, and characteristics into residences in order to:

- Make the residence usable by the greatest number of people
- Respond to the changing needs of the resident
- Improve marketability of the residence"

The *Universal Design Handbook* prescribes the following design guidelines:[11]

1. Finished hallways should be 42" wide
2. All doorways, including closet doors and entry doors, should be 32" wide at minimum. Specifications for entry platforms are also included
3. Ground level and elevator accessible units must have a minimum of one full universally designed bathroom
4. Single lever or ADA-approved faucets must be installed at all sinks, showers, and tubs
5. Electrical outlets have to be installed at a minimum height of 15" and light switches, fan switches and thermostats at a maximum height of 48"
6. All units must have at least one universally designed bedroom on the ground level or elevator accessible floor

Specifications for exterior accessibility, including parking areas and walkways, are also included and, as an acknowledgment of the fact that more and more members of the population own and regularly use personal computers, cabling for high-speed internet access is also required.

Tying Universal Design Policy to Funding Resources

There are several ways that universal design guidelines are promoted at the federal, state, and local levels. Federal regulations, for example, set accessibility standards for large, new or rehabilitated multifamily housing built with the help of federal funds, but not for smaller projects. Some states, such as Georgia, and cities, such as Irvine, CA, have developed their own accessibility guidelines that builders and developers may voluntarily adopt, although these guidelines apply mostly to privately funded projects. In Kentucky, the Kentucky Housing Corporation has tied its universal design policy to its housing finance programs. Thus KHC universal design requirements are mandatory for any projects that receive debt or subsidy financing from KHC equal to 50 percent or more of the total cost of new construction (or reconstruction) of single-family or multi-family housing. The Department of Design and Construction Review offers a full array of technical assistance and likes to begin working with developers right from the inception of the project to ensure that they are meeting all building requirements, including the universal design guidelines. Once the project is built, the Department's inspectors inspect the buildings and certify them.

Many developers and builders around the country have been reluctant to incorporate universal design features into their projects because they believe the cost is prohibitive. Consumers buying new homes are also reluctant to request the features because they fear these features will add substantially to the cost of the housing.[12] But several studies have shown that the added cost of universal design features is very modest. In Kentucky, KHC's Department of Design and Construction Review has polled developers of multifamily and single-family dwellings and has found that, as a result of its Universal Design Policy, additional building costs for a two-bedroom unit are between $900 and $1,500. "Retrofitting," or renovating, homes after they are built to accommodate the occupants' changing physical needs is considerably more expensive.

According to the Department of Design and Construction Review, since the Universal Design Policy went into effect in 2003, at least 500 units have been built that meet universal design requirements.

Success Stories

Housing corporations around the U.S. have given thousands of Americans access to affordable housing. In the past 31 years, Kentucky Housing Corporation has helped countless families find affordable rental housing, and its homeownership programs have assisted over 55,000 families in becoming homeowners, making Kentucky's home ownership rate (74 percent) considerably higher than the overall national rate of 67.8 percent, according to 2001 U.S. Census data. Whether they own or rent, not only do more people have access to affordable housing, with KHC's Universal Design Policy in full effect, they will have housing that will meet their needs for a long time to come. Here are a couple of examples of recent projects built according to the Universal Design Policy guidelines.

- Hilton and Lively Partnership is a builder of affordable housing in central and western Kentucky, and many of their clients are single parents, seniors, and people with disabilities. Hilton and Lively receives some financing through KHC, so it has to comply with KHC's Universal Design Policy. The firm works with manufactured housing, which does not normally incorporate universal design principles, such as wider hallways, generous space in bathrooms, and so on. But it has found a housing manufacturer willing to revise their construction plans to meet the universal design requirements and the firm is standing behind the quality of the homes they build by providing warranties, construction reinforcements, a traditional-looking roof pitch, a permanent foundation, and higher insulation standards compared to other similar homes.
  Hilton and Lively's most recently funded project, the Hilton and Lively Homeownership Program, is building affordable (manufactured) housing with the basic features of universal design in Grayson County's Big Clifty. The project received KHC financing through the HOME Investment Partnership Program and the Housing Development Fund.
- Another project built with funds from the HOME Investment Partnerships Program is the South Main Street Apartments in Edmonton, Kentucky, which will serve older people with incomes at or below 50 percent of the average median income for the area, which is currently $32,500 a year. Funds from the state's Small MultiFamily Affordable Loan Program (SMAL) were also used to build the one-story, 11-unit complex.

End Notes

[1] *Opening Doors: Using the Low income Tax Credit Program to Create Affordable Housing for People with Disabilities*. Emily Cooper and Ann O'Hara. 2005. Available at: http://www.c-c-d.org/od-April05.htm

[2] Ibid.

[3] Ibid.

[4] S. 859. Oct. 26, 2005 Sens. John Ensign, R-Nev., John Kerry, D-Mass., Rick Santorum, R-Pa., and Debbie Stabenow, D-Mich., today sent a 'Dear Colleague' letter to Senate Finance Committee Chairman Charles Grassley, R-Iowa, and Ranking Member Max Baucus, D-

Mont., in support of including a modified version of the Community Development Homeownership Tax Credit Act, as proposed in S. 859 , in the tax package being developed to help rebuild the Gulf Coast. April, 20, 2005 Referred to Senate committee. Status: Read twice and referred to the Committee on Finance.

[5] http://www.kyhousing.org/about/mission.cfm

[6] www.kyhousing.org/about/HPAC.cfm

[7] Ibid.

[8] "Invitation to Apply for….", p.3.

[9] Kentucky 2001 Real Choice Systems Change Grant.

[10] Kentucky Housing Corporation, Department of Design & Construction Review (July 2003) Universal Design Handbook.

[11] More details on these specifications are included in the *Universal Design Handbooks*. Certain exemptions are allowed.

[12] Livable Communities for Adults with Disabilities, Available at http://www.ncd.gov/newsroom/publications/2004/LivableCommunities.htm

In: Creating Livable Communities for People... ISBN: 978-1-60741-534-3
Editor: Alise Vanags

Chapter 4

STRATEGY THREE: AGREEMENT ON COMMON PERFORMANCE MEASURES ACROSS MULTIPLE FEDERALLY FUNDED PROGRAMS

National Council on Disability

There is an enormous variety of programs that are designed to help older people and people with disabilities live independently in the community. But how effective are these programs? Do they respond to people's actual needs and support their aspirations? Strategy Three is one way to begin addressing these questions. The initiatives illustrating this approach have developed tools that facilitate measurement of performance and outcomes. These tools can be applied to a variety of programs that serve people with disabilities and older people.

THE PROGRAM ASSESSMENT RATING TOOL (PART)

The Office of Management and Budget (OMB) developed the Program Assessment Rating Tool (PART) to assess and improve program performance so that the Federal Government can achieve better results with its programs. A PART review helps identify a program's strengths and weaknesses to inform funding and management decisions aimed at making the program more effective. PART therefore looks at factors that affect and reflect program performance, including program purpose and design; performance measurement, evaluations, and strategic planning; program management; and program results. PART allows programs to show improvement over time. It also allows comparisons between similar programs because it includes a consistent series of analytical questions.

PART's current approach to individual program evaluation is just a starting point, however. To effectively measure programs that serve people with disabilities, the system must also evaluate the real impact that these programs have on the people they serve as well as the extent of collaboration among federal agencies to advance the overall goals of social and economic independence and community inclusion for people with disabilities. To achieve these valued outcomes, federal agencies will need to improve coordination across program lines to:

- Provide affordable, appropriate, accessible housing;
- Ensure accessible, affordable, reliable, safe transportation;
- Adjust the physical environment for inclusiveness and accessibility;
- Provide work, volunteer, and education opportunities;
- Ensure access to key health and support services; and
- Encourage participation in civic, cultural, and recreational activities.[1]

When agencies and programs coordinate and work together, it is more likely that these desired results will be achieved.

Program Background

In July 2002, Mitch Daniels, Director of the Office of Management and Budget, announced the PART program as a tool for formally evaluating the effectiveness of federal programs. Mr. Daniels said that this "program assessment effort presents an opportunity to inform and improve agency GPRA [Government Performance and Results Act of 1993] plans and reports, and establish a meaningful systematic link between GPRA and the budget process."[2]

OMB's guidance describes PART as part of a "systematic method of assessing the performance of program activities across the Federal Government."

Program Description

Overview of the Program Structure

PART is a rating tool designed to hold agencies accountable for accomplishing results. PART is a diagnostic tool and the main objective of the PART review is to improve program performance. PART assessments help link performance to budget decisions and provide a basis for making recommendations to improve results. Programs are rated from effective to ineffective, and the ratings and specific findings produced are used to make decisions regarding budgets and policy.

PART places the burden of proving effectiveness with the federal managers responsible for operating the program under review. The PART program provides meaningful evidence to Congress and other decision-makers to help inform funding decisions and identify flaws in underlying statutes that undermine effectiveness.

History

Previous administrations grappled with how to hold federal programs and federal managers accountable.

- President Johnson launched his Planning, Programming, and Budgeting System in 1966 to "substantially improve our ability to decide among competing proposals for funds and to evaluate actual performance." The system was the first serious effort to link budgets to getting results and a form of it remains in use at the Pentagon today.[3]
- President Nixon followed with an effort called Management By Objective. This attempted to identify the goals of federal programs to make it easier to determine what results were expected of each program and where programs were redundant or ineffective. President Nixon stated, "By abandoning programs that have failed, we do not close our eyes to the problems that exist; we shift resources to more productive use."[4]
- President Carter attempted to introduce a concept known as zero-based budgeting in 1977 to force each government program to prove its value each year. "[I]t's not enough to have created a lot of government programs. Now we must make the good programs more effective and improve or weed out those which are wasteful or

unnecessary," President Carter stated in his 1979 State of the Union Address.[5]

- President Clinton's Administration also offered a broad agenda to "reinvent" government to make it cost less and do more.[6]

Thus far the most significant advance in bringing accountability to government programs is the Government Performance and Results Act of 1993. This law requires federal agencies to identify both long-term and annual goals, collect performance data, and justify budget requests based on this data. For example, in the 2003 budget, the Bush Administration rated approximately 130 federal programs on their effectiveness. This first-ever attempt to directly rate program effectiveness was only a start. Since the criteria used to rate programs were not uniform and ratings were based on limited information, its influence on budget decisions was limited.

How it Works

PART is composed of a series of questions designed to provide a consistent approach to rating programs across the Federal Government, relying on objective data to assess programs across a range of issues related to performance. PART also examines factors that the program or agency may not directly control but may be able to influence. For example, if statutory provisions impede effectiveness, legislative changes may be proposed. The formalization of performance assessments through this process is intended to develop defensible and consistent program ratings.

PART is a questionnaire, and evaluation proceeds through four critical areas of assessment–purpose and design, strategic planning, management, and results and accountability.

The questions that comprise PART are generally written in a "Yes/No" response format. They require the user to explain the answer briefly and to include relevant supporting evidence. Responses must be evidence-based and not rely on impressions or generalities. A "yes" answer must be definite and reflect a high standard of performance. Where hard evidence is unavailable, assessments rely more on professional judgment. No one question determines a program's assessment; and in some instances, "not applicable" may be an appropriate answer.

The first set of questions gauges whether the program's design and purpose are clear and defensible. The second section involves strategic planning and weighs whether the agency sets valid annual and long-term goals for programs. The third section rates agency management of programs, including financial oversight and program improvement efforts. The fourth set of questions focuses on results that programs can report with accuracy and consistency.

PART's approximately 30 questions (the number varies depending on the type of program being evaluated) ask for information that responsible federal managers should be able to provide. For instance:

- Is the program designed to have a significant impact in addressing the intended interest, problem, or need?
- Are federal managers and program partners (grantees, sub-grantees, contractors, etc.) held accountable for cost, schedule, and performance results?
- Has the program taken meaningful steps to address its management deficiencies?
- Does the program have a limited number of specific, ambitious long-term performance goals that focus on outcomes and meaningfully reflect the purpose of the program?
- Does the program (including program partners) achieve its annual performance goals?

The answers to questions in each of the four sections result in a numeric score for each section ranging from 0 to 100 (100 being the best). These scores are then combined to achieve an overall qualitative rating that ranges from "effective," to "moderately effective," to "adequate," to "ineffective." Programs that do not have acceptable performance measures or have not yet collected performance data generally receive a rating of "results not demonstrated."

While single, weighted scores can be calculated, the value of reporting, say, an overall 46 out of 100 can be misleading. Reporting a single numerical rating could suggest false precision, or draw attention away from the very areas most in need of improvement. In fact, PART is best seen as a complement to traditional management techniques, and can be used to stimulate a constructive dialogue between program managers, budget analysts, and policy officials. PART serves its purpose if it produces an honest starting point for spending decisions, but it is meant to enrich budget analysis, not replace it. The relationship between an overall PART rating and the budget is not a rigid calculation. Lower ratings do not automatically translate into less funding for a program, just as higher ratings do not automatically translate into higher funding for a program.

How PART Results are Used

PART provides Congress and other stakeholders with important insights into the operation of various programs. It also informs OMB and agency budget decisions, however it is not the only information used in making budgetary decisions. PART is published as part of the President's budget.[7]

Lessons Learned

Over half of the programs analyzed in the first performance assessment received a rating of "results not demonstrated" because of the lack of performance measures and/or performance data. The vast majority of programs have measures that emphasize outputs (such as the number of brochures printed) rather than outcomes or results.

Overall, grant programs received lower than average ratings, suggesting a need for greater emphasis on grantee accountability in achieving overall program goals. Programs found to have inadequate measures had to focus on developing adequate measures and collecting the necessary data before the evaluations were done for 2005. OMB states: "Programs that have not yet been evaluated can anticipate such scrutiny and assess the measures they currently have, and improve them where necessary."

Example

The initial PART found that the vast majority of programs are using measures that emphasize outputs rather than outcomes or results. The Department of Health and Human Services' Ryan White program ensures care and treatment for people with HIV through assistance to localities disproportionately affected by HIV. The program funding goes directly to the states and other public/private/non-profit entities. Through PART it was discovered that the program only measured the number of people it served; in the future it will also measure health outcomes, such as the number of deaths from HIV/AIDS.[8]

2004 Summary Example: The Ryan White Program[9]

Program: *Ryan White*

Agency: *Department of Health and Human Services*
Bureau: *Health Resources and Services Administration*

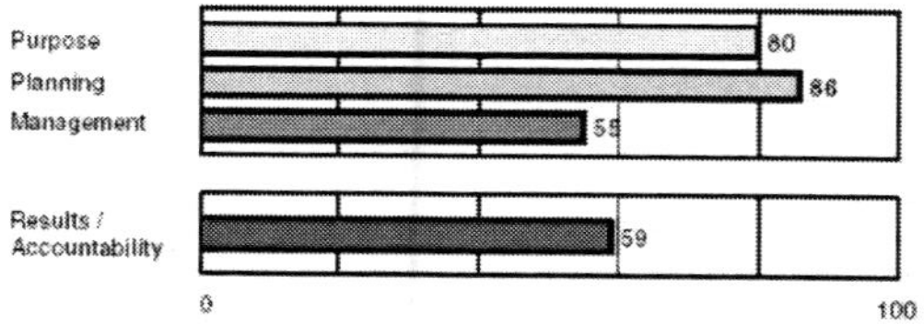

☐ Results Achieved
☐ Results Not Demonstrated
☑ Measures Adequate
☐ New Measures Needed

Key Performance Measures	*Year*	*Target*	*Actual*
Long-term Measure: National rate of deaths per 100,000 people due to HIV infection (New measure)	1994		15.4
	1999		5.4
	2010	3.6	
Long-term Measure: National proportion of people living with HIV receiving primary medical care and treatment (New measure)	2000		33%
	2010	50%	
Annual Measure: Number of persons who learn their serostatus from Ryan White CARE Act-funded programs (New measure)	2000		352,283
	2004	381,323	

Rating: *Adequate*

Program Type: *Block / Formula Grants*

Program Summary:

The Ryan White program ensures care and treatment for persons with HIV through assistance to localities disproportionately affected by HIV. The funding goes to States, and other public/private/nonprofit entities.

The assessment found:
1. The program has developed new long-term and annual performance goals.
2. There is effective coordination with similar programs, regular independent evaluations occur, and the Health Resources and Service Administration (HRSA) is working with Booz Allen Hamilton to identify and manage areas in need of organizational improvement.
2. There is general consensus that the program purpose is clear and the program addresses a specific problem. The score for the program design portion of this section was affected by weaknesses with program design. The statute allows duplication among services funded under each Title and funding allocations are based on a formula that provides funds according to the number of AIDS cases over a 5 year period without regard to the level of sickness or need of those living with HIV/AIDS.
3. The program has contributed to the overall decline in the number of AIDS cases and deaths due to HIV. Program results were considerably affected by the fact that in some cases baseline data are not yet available and evaluations could focus more on the results of the program.
4. HRSA has not implemented preemptive mechanisms to identify problems or make corrective fixes prior to the mismanagement of resources. Some grantees/subgrantees do not use their funds according to the terms of their award. When problems are identified, legal action is taken, funds are returned, and/or individuals pay restitution.

In response to these findings the Administration will:
1. Develop recommendations and legislative strategies in preparation for the 2005 reauthorization, to find more meaningful ways of allocating drug treatment funding and standardizing eligibility across states.
2. Increase funding for the Ryan White AIDS Drug Assistance Program, +$100 million, so that the program can purchase drug treatments for an additional 9,200 persons.

(For more information on this program, please see the Department of Health and Human Services chapter in the Budget volume.)

Program Funding Level (in millions of dollars)

2002 Actual	2003 Estimate	2004 Estimate
1,910	1,911	2,010

PART and People with Disabilities

In 2004, the President's Committee for People with Intellectual Disabilities (PCPID) released *A Charge We Have to Keep: A Road Map to Personal and Economic Freedom for Persons with Intellectual Disabilities in the 21st Century*. In the Road Map, PCPID identified a weakness in PART, namely that there are no measures that evaluate collaboration among related programs across federal agencies. There is also no assessment of agency activity to partner with the private sector and leverage resources to reduce dependence on government. PCPID explains that such measures would: "reveal the degree of an existing or total absence of a fluid continuity among agencies and programs. Continuity is very important for people with intellectual disabilities, for their disability or condition continues throughout their lifespan–from early family life, to education, to employment, to community living, and, finally, to retirement and end of life."[10]

A single agency or program may appear successful in accordance with PART, but that particular agency or program may fail for people with disabilities because it does not, for example, provide the kind of continuity described above. The PCPID recommendation urges that OMB "consider the life span of people with intellectual disabilities when assessing agencies and programs."[11]

Conclusion

With proper performance measures in place, federal programs that have an impact on the lives of people with disabilities can be redirected from outcomes that perpetuate poverty, dependence, and absence of personal freedom to valued results that lead to greater self-sufficiency, employment, and personal freedom.

The PART program can be used to create "a new culture of measurement and accountability that raises expectations for policymakers, service providers, parents, and individuals with disabilities.

In order for PART to be most effective and, simultaneously, benefit people with disabilities in the areas of housing, transportation, physical environment, work opportunities, health and social services, and engagement in community life, the current approach for evaluating programs through PART must be enhanced to measure the programs' real impact on people's lives and the extent to which agencies collaborate with one another to achieve the desired outcomes.

Resources

Office of Management and Budget's PART homepage available at http://www.whitehouse.gov/omb/part/index.html

Office of Management and Budget, Executive Office of the President, Budget of the United States Government: Creating a Better Government: Improving Government Performance; Fiscal Year 2002, at 11-14 (2001), available at: http://www.whitehouse.gov/omb/budget/fy2002/budget.pdf .

PART Training slides. Available at: http://www.whitehouse.gov/omb/part/fy2005/2005_training_slides.pdf .

Introduction to PART, *Rating the Performance of Federal Programs,* available at:
http://www.gpoaccess.gov/usbudget/fy04/pdf/budget/ performance.pdf .

PART Frequently Asked Questions, available at: http://www.whitehouse.gov/omb/part/2004_faq.html .

President's Committee for People with Intellectual Disabilities. *A Charge We Have to Keep: A Road Map to Personal and Economic Freedom for Persons with Intellectual Disabilities in the 21st Century*. (2004).

Measuring Results: Learning from the Administration on Aging—State Collaboration to Develop Model Performance Outcome Measurement Systems

The Administration on Aging (AoA) was created with the passage of the Older Americans Act, signed into law by President Lyndon B. Johnson on July 14, 1965 and reauthorized on November 13, 2000. With a yearly budget of approximately $1.3 billion, AoA is part of a federal, state, tribal, and local partnership network that serves about 7 million older persons and their caregivers. AoA consists of 56 State Units on Aging, 655 Area Agencies on

Aging, 233 Tribal and Native organizations, two organizations that provide services to Native Hawaiians, 29,000 service providers, and thousands of volunteers. AoA provides federal administration of community services programs that are mandated under the Older Americans Act, such as nutrition, transportation, and health promotion services, elder abuse prevention, and family caregiver support. AoA also awards funds to support research, demonstration, and training programs.

AoA is sponsoring an initiative to develop and field test a core set of performance measures for state and community programs on aging operating under Title III of the Older Americans Act. Called the Performance Outcomes Measure Project (POMP), this initiative helps states and Area Agencies on Aging (AoA) address their own planning and performance reporting needs, while assisting AoA to meet the accountability provisions of the Government Performance and Results Act (GPRA) and the Office of Management and Budget's program assessment requirements using the Program Assessment Rating Tool (PART).

Background: The AoA Performance Outcomes Measure Project (POMP)

POMP was initiated in response to the growing importance of collecting timely, accurate, and comparable data as a result of GPRA and the advent of PART, as well as related state and local initiatives that link continued funding to demonstrated program benefits and outcomes. While output information describes programs, clients, and services, the Government Performance and Results Act actually requires information about program *outcomes*, that is, information about how services received have helped the people who receive them and how funding for service systems is used to improve and modernize those systems.

In order to measure service outcomes on the local level, AoA developed POMP in partnership with the National Association of State Units on Aging and the National Association of Area Agencies on Aging. The main objective of the project is to develop and field-test performance outcome measures suitable for ongoing use by local agencies and AoA in determining the effectiveness of aging networks and the services they provide.

These measures emphasize individual outcomes related to the health and psycho-social state of the people who are served, including their nutritional risk, physical functioning, emotional well-being, social functioning, and satisfaction with the services they receive. Other measures look at the benefits of services that support caregivers and the degree to which people are satisfied with the home care services they receive. Measures are also being developed to capture the performance of the aging network in reducing barriers to services and building the capacity of the aging services system.

Key Features of the Project

Since the inception of the project, area agencies in more than twenty states have received funding from the AoA to collaborate on the POMP project. AoA has contracted with researchers to help develop data collection instruments in each of the measurement areas that draw on the best research available. The participating agencies are full partners in the development of these instruments and are participating in the field-testing of the performance outcome measures. A national research corporation under contract with AoA provides technical assistance to project sites in data collection methodology, tools for uniform data storage and transfer, and data analysis services for project sites and AoA.

The POMP data collection instruments are essentially survey questionnaires that are administered by the participating agencies in their locales using sampling methodology, rather than collecting information from each person who participates in their programs. With the participation of the AoA grantees, performance measurement surveys have been developed for the following service areas:

- Caregivers
- Congregate Nutrition Program
- Homemaker Service
- Home Delivered Nutrition Program
- Information and Assistance Assessment
- Transportation Service
- Case Management
- Senior Centers

In addition, survey instruments were designed to document client characteristics, such as physical functioning, social functioning, emotional well-being, and demographic information.

Using these standardized survey instruments, the individual grantees are responsible for conducting the surveys with their own service recipients (usually through telephone interviews), sharing the data with AoA, and participating in the refinement of existing measures and the development of any new ones. Through their participation in the program, grantees learn sampling techniques and methodologies for data collection and analysis, which are generally not widespread within the aging network.

The National POMP

Because the initial focus of POMP was to develop outcome measures and test them for *local* program assessment, the findings from data collected by the individual grantees cannot be generalized. This initial period of the program allowed for the development and testing of data collection instruments, sampling procedures and methods, and information collection processes and procedures, and provided the local grantees with valuable information about the outcomes of service provision in their communities.

AoA is now using the tools developed in the initial, local stage of the program to measure outcomes nationally. To date, AoA has conducted two *national* surveys employing the performance outcome measures developed so far in the program in order to evaluate, *from a consumer perspective,* whether its programs are meeting the needs of the older people they serve. For example, looking at one of its key service areas—nutrition—the national surveys help AoA determine:

- The extent to which aging networks target services to elderly individuals at high nutritional risk
- The extent to which nutritional risk is improved as a result of AoA meals programs
- Overall consumer satisfaction with meals programs provided through the network

Similar types of information are solicited through the surveys for the other areas of interest, such as transportation services, information and assistance services, home care services, and caregiver support services.

Through POMP, AoA is developing a performance outcomes measurement system that:

- Truly focuses on outcomes rather than the usual outputs

- Involves (and even depends on) local service providers as key partners in outcomes evaluation
- Standardizes measures so that they can be used across local sites as well as nationally to assess the impact of AoA programs on the lives of people they serve
- Through initial surveys, establishes benchmarks against which future assessments can be compared to track progress over time
- Establishes performance targets for future annual performance plans

More information, as well as the survey instruments, can be found at www.gpra.net.

Federal Interagency Forum on Aging-Related Statistics: A Collaborative Effort to Measure the Well-Being of People Aged 65+

The Administration on Aging is one of several federal agencies that have been collaborating since 1986 to establish and report on a set of key indicators that describe the overall status of the U.S. population age 65 and over.

The other collaborating agencies include the:

- U.S. Census Bureau
- Agency for Healthcare Research and Quality
- Centers for Disease Control and Prevention
- Centers for Medicare and Medicaid Services
- National Institutes of Health
- Office of the Assistant Secretary for Planning and Evaluation
- Bureau of Labor Statistics
- Department of Veterans Affairs
- Environmental Protection Agency
- Office of Management and Budget
- Social Security Administration

The Forum has so far published two reports (one in 2000, the other in 2004) entitled, Older Americans: Key Indicators of Well-Being, that bring together federal statistics from over a dozen national data sources to monitor several important areas in the lives of older Americans—population, economics, health status, health risks and behaviors, and health care. The reports provide a broad summary of indicators of well-being for the U.S. population aged 65 and over and monitor changes in these indicators over time. By examining a broad range of indicators, researchers, policymakers, service providers, and the Federal Government can better understand the areas of well-being that are improving for older Americans and the areas of well-being that require more attention and effort.

These reports are available at: http://www.agingstats.gov

End Notes

[1] These are the six areas that define livable communities for people with disabilities. National Council on Disability. *Livable Communities for Adults with Disabilities.* (December 2, 2004). p8. Available at: http://www.ncd.gov/newsroom/publications/2004/LivableCommunities.htm

[2] Government Performance Management. "OMB's Program Assessment Rating Tool (PART)." Available at: http://www.john-mercer.com/omb_part.htm

[3] Office of Management and Budget. "FY 2004 Budget Chapter Introducing the PART: Rating the Performance of Federal Programs." (2004). Available at: http://www.gpoaccess.gov/usbudget/fy04/pdf/budget/performance.pdf/

[4] Ibid.

[5] Ibid.

[6] Ibid.

[7] Office of Management and Budget. "Program Rating Assessment Tool: Training Slides." (2004). Available at: http://www.whitehouse.gov/omb/part/ fy2005/2005_training_slides.pdf

[8] See note 19.

[9] Available at: http://www.whitehouse.gov/omb/budget/fy2004/pma/ryanwhite.pdf#search='Ryan%20White% 20Program '

[10] President's Committee for People with Intellectual Disabilities. *A Charge We Have to Keep: A Road Map to Personal and Economic Freedom for Persons with Intellectual Disabilities in the 21st Century.* (2004). p19. Available at: http://www.acf.hhs.gov/ programs/pcpid/2004_rpt_pres/2004_report.html

[11] Ibid.

In: Creating Livable Communities for People... ISBN: 978-1-60741-534-3
Editor: Alise Vanags

Chapter 5

STRATEGY FOUR: UTILIZATION OF PRIVATE SECTOR MATCH TO COMPETITIVELY SECURE PUBLIC FUNDING AND STIMULATE PUBLIC-PRIVATE SECTOR PARTNERSHIPS

National Council on Disability

Livable communities ensure that all residents, regardless of ability, are able to participate in the community's economic, civic, and social life. The examples included under Strategy Four illustrate how public-private sector partnerships can promote asset development and financial independence among people with low incomes and people with disabilities. When people with low incomes and people with disabilities are able to accumulate income to continue their education, buy homes, and/or start businesses, they not only enrich their own lives, they help support the economy of the communities in which they live.

INDIVIDUAL DEVELOPMENT ACCOUNTS

Among adults with disabilities, 34% live in households with a total income of $15,000 or less (compared to only 12% of those without disabilities), and approximately 70% of people with disabilities are unemployed.[1] In a recent Harris Survey poll, 39% of people with disabilities indicated that the lack of financial resources is the most serious problem they face.[2] With such a high unemployment rate, and so little income, people with disabilities, like other low-income families, are the least likely to save money.[3]

Individual Development Accounts (IDAs) are "asset development tools," one of many economic development programs created by Congress over the last few years to provide savings incentives. IDAs are matched savings accounts that help people with low incomes accrue funds for the purpose of purchasing a first home, paying for post-secondary education, or starting a small business. Generally, IDAs are implemented by community-based organizations in partnership with a financial institution that holds the deposit and enable people to be more self-sufficient. Personal savings can be matched by federal and state governments and/or private sector organizations, generally at rates of 1:1, 2:1, or other more generous matches. In addition, an account holder usually receives financial counseling when he or she opens an IDA.

Legislation, passed at the federal and state levels, governs how IDAs operate. Since 1991, at least 500 community-based IDA programs have been developed in 49 of 50 states. An estimated 20,000 IDAs have been established in the U.S.[4]

The IDA program is a successful policy mechanism that has helped thousands of low-income families build their personal assets and invest in their communities and themselves. By facilitating asset building for the purchase of homes, small business development, and higher education, IDA programs have helped people with disabilities and other low-income families live more independently and contribute to their communities' economy in the same ways that millions of other citizens do.

Background

Asset accumulation programs first emerged as part of U.S. domestic policy in the 1970s with the creation of savings vehicles such as IRAs, Roth IRAs, and 401(k)s. These programs, targeted to middle and upper income workers, provide savings incentives through tax relief.[5]

In the late 1980s, Michael Sherraden offered a new theory of welfare based on assets, and an asset–building tool he dubbed IDAs. Sherraden proposed IDAs as private, long-term accounts established at birth, by public funds, and available to every person in the country. IDAs are like 401(k)s, except that 1) IDAs use matching deposits instead of tax breaks as the incentive to save, and 2) people saving in an IDA do so with the help of a non-profit organization that usually requires economic literacy training.[6]

It was not until the welfare reform efforts by the Clinton Administration and Congress in the mid-1990s that enthusiasm for IDAs was generated. IDA savings products are now created under various Federal programs aimed to broaden their applicability. The U.S. Treasury Department's Bank Enterprise Awards program and various initiatives under the Community Reinvestment Act are two examples. There are also IDA-like vehicles, such as Family Self-Sufficiency Accounts, administered by public housing authorities around the country and sponsored by the U.S. Department of Housing and Urban Development (HUD). In addition, 44 states have some type of IDA policy or initiative targeting a wide variety of low-income households.[7]

Historical Progression of IDAs, Barriers, and Solutions

Initially, several barriers hindered IDA participation by low-income people with disabilities. Before 1996, people receiving Supplemental Security Income (SSI) could not participate in IDAs. The Social Security Act states that individuals are not eligible for SSI disability benefits if they have more than $2,000 in countable assets, and couples are ineligible if they have more than $3,000 in assets. Assets accrued in IDAs would make people ineligible for SSI disability benefits, thus eliminating any incentive to open an IDA. This barrier was overcome when Congress passed the Personal Responsibility and Work Reconciliation Act of 1996 (PWORA). PWORA authorized states to create community-based IDA programs with Temporary Assistance for Needy Families (TANF) block grant funds. This legislation allowed money saved in IDAs to be disregarded when determining eligibility for means-tested government assistance programs such as SSI.[8]

A second perceived barrier to IDA participation by some policy analysts and advocates is the earned income requirement. The Assets for Independence Act (AFIA), Section 408—Eligibility for Participation, currently requires that an individual have earned income in order to participate in IDA programs. The majority of people who receive SSI and/or Social Security Disability Insurance (SSDI) want to work, yet not all are able to work full- or part-time. Leydorf & Kaplan (2001) proposed allowing people receiving SSI and/or SSDI to set aside a portion of their benefits and/or other non-earned income (e.g., gifts) in an IDA to help them enter or return to work and achieve economic productivity.

The three main types of IDAs are TANF IDAs, Assets for Independence Act (AFIA) IDAs, and "non-TANF, non-AFIA" IDAs. Both TANF IDAs and AFIA IDAs are federally funded and are excluded from federal benefit program asset limits. Non-TANF, non-AFIA IDAs are those that rely on state, local, or private funds, and may be counted as assets in determining eligibility for government benefit programs (IDA State Policy Briefs, Vol. 1, No. 2).

In an effort to test the efficacy of IDA programs, the Corporation for Enterprise Development (CFED) launched the Downpayment on the American Dream Policy Demonstration (ADD) in September 1997.[9,10] This five-year demonstration sought to assess the number of participants, longevity of participation, patterns of savings, and amounts saved, as well as the uses of IDAs, whether for homeownership, education, employment, or other uses. ADD brought together 13 community-based organizations[11] from around the country to design, implement, and administer IDA initiatives in their communities. At completion, 2,364 IDAs were established in low-income and asset-poor communities. Findings from ADD showed that the average monthly net deposits per participant were $19.07. The average participant saved 50 percent of the monthly savings target and made deposits in 6 of 12 months. Participants accumulated an average of $700 per year including matches. Notably, deposits increased as the monthly target increased.[12] In addition, ADD succeeded in expanding the field of community-based IDA programs around the country by serving as the successful model for federally funded IDAs under the Assets for Independence Act (AFIA).[13]

A key factor in making IDAs successful is economic education. Financial literacy helped IDA participants reach their goals and become better integrated into the mainstream economic system. IDA involvement has also been shown to influence participants' "confidence about the future, willingness to defer gratification, avoidance of risky behavior, and investment in community."[14]

IDAs benefit communities as funds are reinvested right back into the community. The ADD graduates reinvested their savings in the community as follows: 28% used their savings to purchase a home, 23% to start or expand a small business, 21% for higher education, and the remainder for home repair, job training, or retirement.[15] By December 2001, the 2,364 ADD participants had accrued $36,481,498 in savings, including matching funds with monthly deposits ranging from $30–$75. Startup costs averaged $70 per participant per month; after startup, expenses averaged $45 per participant per month. These costs are well worthwhile–the Corporation for Enterprise Development (CFED) "estimates that each federal dollar invested in IDAs would yield a return of approximately five dollars to the national economy in the form of new businesses, additional earnings, new and rehabilitated homes, reduced welfare expenditures, and human capital associated with greater educational attainment."[16]

Thus, IDAs yield many benefits, including economic household stability, higher educational attainment, increased health and satisfaction, increased civic involvement, and decreased risk of intergenerational poverty transmission.[17]

How IDAs Work

Table 3 identifies the key players and activities that comprise a typical IDA program. Each IDA program has a sponsoring organization with dedicated staff who, usually through multiple partnerships with financial institutions and training providers, coordinate and carry out IDA program activities that include raising matching and administrative funds, developing marketing and outreach materials, recruiting accountholders and opening accounts, providing training and counseling, administering matching funds, and collecting and managing account transaction data. It is important to note that the division of labor among key players varies widely. This is in part because IDA programs are uniquely designed in accordance with the structure and available resources of the sponsoring organization, as well as the specific needs of the target population.[18]

Once recruited, account holders participate in what is usually a four-stage process. While the order of these stages may vary from one program to another, the sequence outlined is most common:

1. **Introduction and orientation**. In a one-on-one or small group session conducted by the sponsoring organization, prospective accountholders typically learn about asset-building theory, how savings accumulate through compounding interest and how assets appreciate over time, how the IDA program is structured and administered, who is eligible to participate, and what asset purchases are permissible.[19]

2. **Opening accounts.** After attending the orientation, participants open a savings account with the partnering financial institution.[20]

3. **Financial education and asset training.** Usually early in the IDA program, accountholders are required to attend financial education classes that cover diverse topics such as household budgeting, personal financial management, establishing and repairing credit, goal setting, and principles of investing. Some programs also provide specialized training classes for one or more permissible asset purchases. Others provide counseling and related services.[21]

4. **Withdrawal and asset purchase.** As accountholders reach their incremental or ultimate savings goals and identify their desired assets, they make approved withdrawals and purchase assets. Once assets are purchased, accountholders will either continue to save in their IDA or will transition to a standard savings account or other mainstream financial product.[22]

Lessons Learned

The following lessons have been gleaned from ADD and other IDA programs:

1. **Accumulation period.** The accumulation period refers to the number of months after opening an account that participants may make deposits that are eligible for matching funds. While IDAs were not originally envisioned as time-limited instruments, limited resources and the need to demonstrate results have made accumulation periods necessary. However, organizations must be sure that the accumulation period provides enough time for individuals to develop regular savings behaviors and accumulate the funds necessary to achieve their individual asset goals.[23]

2. **Monthly savings target.** Instituting a minimum monthly savings target aids accountholders in establishing regular savings behavior. Most programs serving adults have minimum monthly deposits between $20 and $50 per month.[24]

3. **Match cap.** The IDA match cap or ceiling is the maximum amount an individual's account will be matched. IDA programs have found annual or lifetime (i.e., total amount based on duration of the

program) match caps most effective. Those who wish to encourage greater savings through lump-sum deposits (such as income tax returns) and reinforce savings behavior tend to set an annual maximum IDA match cap that is more than the minimum monthly deposit for 12 months. For instance, if the minimum monthly deposit is $25, an accountholder making regular deposits would save $300. If the matching rate were 1:1, the total IDA would be $600 at the end of 1 year. However, if the annual IDA match cap is $600, there is an incentive for extra saving beyond the monthly minimum or a planned deposit of anticipated lump sums.[25]

4. **Matching rate.** There is still a great deal to learn about the relationship between matching rates and participant behavior. Surveys of and interviews with accountholders indicate that the matching rate initially attracts individuals to an IDA program. Higher matching rates seem to reduce the risk of participants making unauthorized, unmatched withdrawals and encourage accountholders to keep higher balances; they do not, however, seem to lead to larger deposits.[26]

5. **Wait period.** Many programs institute a wait period of some number of weeks after enrollment before a matched withdrawal is allowed. This wait period serves to ensure that accountholders are not saving before they are ready to save and also promotes the accumulation of funds and development of good savings habits before withdrawal.[27]

6. **Financial literacy education.** Almost all IDA programs require accountholders to complete a certain number of hours of general financial education; some programs require that classes be initiated before accounts are opened and others require that classes be completed before matched withdrawals are made. The Center for Social Development reports that the number of required hours of general financial education ranges from 6 to 45 among ADD programs, with a mean of 13 hours. Additional data on ADD account holders indicate that savings outcomes improved as the number of hours of financial education completed increased from zero to 12; outcomes leveled off or diminished once the number of hours exceeded 12. More extensive research is needed, however, to better understand the relationship between financial education and savings outcomes in IDA programs.[28]

Individual account ownership is recommended to maximize individual responsibility and choice. Separate, parallel accounts are recommended to simplify accounting and prevent unauthorized withdrawal of matching funds. Monthly account statements allow accountholders to self-monitor savings behavior in accordance with a monthly budget and also serve as an incentive for greater savings by reporting the steady accumulation of matching dollars. Instituting penalties for unmatched withdrawals is viewed by most practitioners as an effective way to encourage saving and discourage withdrawals, although opinions vary as to what type of penalty is most effective. There is also disagreement in the field about what constitutes appropriate permissible uses for matched withdrawals. While home purchase, micro-enterprise, post-secondary education, and job training are seen as appropriate by most (if not all) practitioners, some programs allow one or two uses and rule out others based on their particular resources and expertise. Additionally, some programs allow withdrawals for other purposes–such as home repair or remodeling, purchase of an automobile or computer, retirement, or tuition for summer camp–that they deem appropriate for their specific target population. As a general rule, when determining permissible uses, it is recommended that practitioners not lose sight of the underlying policy goal of IDAs: to incentivize the accumulation of enduring and appreciating assets.[29]

Resources Used to Fund IDAs

The costs of IDA programs are of growing interest to a wide range of IDA stakeholders. New or potential practitioners want to know what it will take to plan and implement their own IDA programs; policymakers want to know how much funding should be allocated to ensure the success of proposed IDA initiatives; private foundations want to know how their contributions are being used by host organizations; evaluators and policy entrepreneurs want to quantify actual program costs to identify ways to increase efficiency and reduce delivery costs so that IDAs can be implemented on a larger scale. While information on IDA program costs is far from complete or conclusive, evaluation data from ADD programs, which represent the longest-running IDA programs, provide insight into what sorts of time and resources are presently required to effectively deliver IDAs.

A thorough cost study of the largest ADD program found the total program costs during the first two years of operation to be $129 per participant-month, or $3.56 for each dollar of participant net deposits.[30]

IMPLEMENTING IDAS IN THE STATES: LEARNING FROM IOWA

Federal IDA-related legislation has influenced state IDA-related legislation, and vice versa. Many states have amended IDA legislation in ways that minimize restrictions and facilitate program delivery across diverse areas, supporting diverse populations. While some states continue to pursue restriction-heavy legislation, the more prominent trend is toward flexible IDA policies that minimize restrictions and facilitate program delivery.

At the present time, there are 24 state-supported IDA programs operating and five programs in the planning stages. These 29 programs are funded by various funding streams, most commonly TANF funds, state general revenue funds, state tax credits, AFIA grant funds, and private funds. State IDA policy has strongly influenced federal IDA policy as well as growth of the IDA field.[31] Significant state contributions to IDA policy include:

1. Exempting the earnings on IDA savings from taxation.
2. Exempting IDA deposits as assets when determining qualifications in state-administered means-tested programs.
3. Allowing IDA uses beyond home ownership, small business capitalization, or college education, such as home repair, car purchase, retirement savings, health care, job training, and job-related expenses (e.g., childcare, work equipment).
4. Establishing IDAs for children, typically for educational expenses.
5. Removing restrictions from early IDA program designs; creating programs that are appealing to special populations, among whom certain restrictions are considered inappropriate.
6. Including Native Americans in program planning and implementation, with special considerations for cultural differences and governance structures of sovereign nations.
7. Identifying and establishing a wide variety of funding streams at the federal, state, and local levels.
8. Establishing the use of tax credits as a funding source for IDAs.

The public and private sectors should look to state IDA policies for creative and innovative ideas to design broader and more inclusive IDA policies.

Iowa[32]

In 1993, Iowa became the first state to pass IDA policy as part of its sweeping welfare reform bill, the State Human Investment Policy (SHIP). SHIP included a provision to establish a five-year IDA demonstration program that would create thousands of IDAs for individuals with low incomes. The first accounts were opened in 1996, and Iowa's legislation became a model for other states desiring to enact IDA policy.

Since 1999, the Institute for Social and Economic Development (ISED) Ventures has administered Iowa's IDA program entitled Iowans Save! Program participants deposit money in special savings accounts that are then matched 1:1 with federal and local funds. Federal match funds are provided by the Assets for Independence Act (AFIA) through the Office of Community Services in the U.S. Department of Health and Human Services (DHHS). Local matching funds are provided by ISED Ventures program partners, the United Way of Central Iowa, and the Iowa Finance Authority.

The Iowans Save! program requires participants to use the funds for first-time home ownership, higher education, or starting/expanding a small business. Eligibility is based on family size and earned income. Participants are required to show proof of earned income that cannot exceed the following guidelines (Table 1):

Table 2 shows how the maximum match amount and the uses of the funds vary by location.

Iowans Save! also has a refugee program that matches every dollar saved with two dollars for a maximum matching contribution of $2,000 per individual and $4,000 per family. The refugee program is more liberal in allowable uses of IDA accounts and allows accountholders to use accumulated funds to buy a car or a computer and make home renovations in addition to the standard uses allowed in the other Iowans Save! program.

The process for enrollment in the program begins with submittal of an application. Qualified applicants attend an orientation program in one of three sites (Des Moines, Waterloo, or Cedar Rapids), and then are ready to sign a savings agreement and open a savings account.

Table 1. Income Guidelines

Family Size	Maximum Earned Income
1	$18,620
2	$24,980
3	$31,340
4	$37,700
5	$44,060
6	$50,420
7	$56,780
8	$63,140

Table 2. Maximum Matches

	Des Moines	Elsewhere in Iowa
Minimum deposit	$25 per month	$25 per month
Match rate	1:1	1:1
Funding sources	DHHS United Way of Central Iowa	DHHS Iowa Finance Authority
Maximum matching contribution	• $2,000 per individual • $4,000 per household	• $1,000 per individual • $1,000 per household
Permissible uses	• First time home ownership • College/vocational training • Start/expand a small business	• First time home ownership

The process for enrollment in the program begins with submittal of an application. Qualified applicants attend an orientation program in one of three sites (Des Moines, Waterloo, or Cedar Rapids), and then are ready to sign a savings agreement and open a savings account.

Depending on the participant's location, matching funds are kept in separate Iowans Save! bank accounts at Bankers Trust in Des Moines or US Bank in Waterloo and Cedar Rapids. Participants receive monthly bank statements that show individual savings, and quarterly bank statements that show the combination of individual savings and matched funds earnings. Participants who neglect to deposit funds for three consecutive months risk being dropped from the program and losing the match dollars. With the permission of an Iowans Save! program manager, emergency withdrawals of individual savings (not match funds) are allowed after 6 months of enrollment. Such withdrawals must be repaid within one year.

Table 3. Key Roles, Players and Activities

Key Role	Possible Players	Possible Activities
Sponsoring organization	Community-based non-profit, faith-based organization, credit union, community development financial institution, United Way agency, tribal organization.	Program design, program administration, outreach and recruitment, enrollment, data collection, account monitoring, counseling.
Funding provider	Private foundations, financial institutions, chambers of commerce, federal agencies, local and state governments.	Provision of planning, administration, matching funds.
Financial institution	Banks, credit unions and community development financial institutions.	Maintain accounts, provide related financial services and products.
Training provider	IDA program sponsor, cooperative extension programs, financial institution staff, financial education specialists, credit counselors, homebuying counselors, financial aid counselors, small business development trainers.	Administer financial literacy education classes, provide asset-specific training.
Accountholder	Welfare recipients, low-wage workers, rural poor, Native Americans, persons with disabilities, senior citizens, immigrants or refugees, youth.	Open accounts, attend education and training classes, deposit funds, withdraw funds, purchase assets.

From: *Boshara, R. (December 2001)* Building Assets: A Report on the Asset-Development and IDA Field. *Washington, DC*: CFED.

The program provides all participants with financial education and purpose-specific training to facilitate sound decision making. "Dollars and Sense Money Management" is a series of free workshops that help participants manage their money and develop personal savings and budget plans. Participants get a confidential credit report and assistance in repairing credit problems (if applicable). "Homeownership Counseling" is a step-by-step program that takes first time home buyers through the entire process of purchasing a home. "Small Business Assistance" assists clients in researching relevant markets, developing business plans, and obtaining low-interest loans. "Higher Education or Vocational Training" helps clients develop educational savings plans.

According to Iowans Save! legislation, for people to be considered eligible for the program, their income must be below 200% of the federal poverty guidelines, or earned income tax credit, or TANF.

While relatively few people with disabilities have taken advantage of the Iowans Save program, the following true story shows how well the program can work for them:

> The success of the Iowans Save! program can best be illustrated with D.L.'s[33] experience. D.L. is paralyzed from the waist down, uses a wheelchair to get around, and rents a 2-story house where she lives with her young son. D.L. heard about the Iowans Save! program from a friend and initially planned to purchase a ranch style home, with all rooms at ground level.
>
> D.L. was employed full time at John Deere Community Credit Union with an annual income below $28,000. In February 2000, she qualified for the IDA program according to Earned Income Tax Credit (EITC) guidelines. Leveraging EITC helps to "jump start" savings for people who find it difficult to save the $25 monthly minimum while making ends meet.[34] D.L. completed the required "Dollars and Sense Money Management" class in March 2000 and the "Homeownership Counseling" class in April 2000. By October 2003, D.L. saved nearly $4,000 and an additional $4,000 in matching funds, but could not find a suitable home within her price range of $80,000.
>
> D.L. was disappointed and considered dropping out of the program altogether (and losing the $4,000 in matching funds). Program staff, however, encouraged D.L. to consider using her funds in other approved ways and, following their advice, D.L. decided to revise her savings goal to open a business with her brother–a jazz club in Valley Junction, West Des Moines, Iowa. In February 2004, D.L. began the legal processes, including obtaining a liquor license, to open the club, and in June 2004 D.L. completed the Iowans Save! program, withdrew her money, and used the funds to open the club, which is still in operation.
>
> While D.L. did not fulfill her original intent to buy a home and continues to rely on family and friends to help her access the second floor, she is now

the co-owner of a business that could help raise her income to the point where she will be able to buy an affordable and accessible home.

Debra Carr, Director of Asset Development and Des Moines Office Development Manager, who provided this story, attributes D.L.'s success to her tenacity and ability to follow through.

The AFIA grant expired in August 2004. From 1999 to 2004, ISED Ventures' citizen IDA program and refugee IDA program helped 1,463 participants save for their futures. The overall impact has been reinvestment of $11,401,063 in the community in the form of purchased homes, education, business start-up, car purchases, computer purchases, and home renovations.

The Future of IDAs

There are several challenges that need to be addressed before IDAs can be implemented on a larger scale:

- **Make Savings Requirements More Flexible.** Current IDA policy is designed for the short-term. Policy and program success is often defined by asset purchases made within a few years of establishing the account.[35] However, not everyone can effectively save according to a prescribed timetable. Policies need to be implemented that allow people with disabilities and other low-income families to save irregularly or deposit less than the minimum monthly amount provided they are saving for homeownership.

- **Support Non-Profit Fundraising Efforts and Program Delivery on the State Level.** States regard IDA programs as public-private partnerships and often expect non-profit partners to raise private or federal funds before state funds are appropriated. However, states rarely assist in fundraising efforts. They provide matching dollars but often do not provide support for such things as program start-up or operating expenses. As a result, this may limit the expansion of IDAs in the states.[36]

- **Connect IDA Programs to Other State or Federal Asset-Building Programs**. For IDA programs to grow, connections between these programs and other state or federal asset-building programs for low-income families must be explored. Such programs could include the Workforce Investment Act, Housing and Urban Development (HUD) Home Funds, and Federal Home Loan Bank (FHLB) Affordable Housing Programs. Forging such connections will require imagination and action on the part of policymakers and advocates, as well as agreement that the goal of giving all people the opportunity to build assets is good for the people and good for the country as a whole.[37]

Additional Resources for More Information

The Center for Social Development at Washington University in St. Louis. http://gwbweb.wustl.edu/csd/

Corporation for Enterprise Development. http://www.cfed.org/

IDA Network. http://www.idanetwork.org/

Administration for Children and Families at the U.S. Department of Health and Human Services. http://www.acf.dhhs.gov/assetbuilding/

Sherraden, M. (1991). *Assets and the Poor: A New American Welfare Policy*. New York: M.E. Sharpe, Inc.

Boshara, R. (2001). The rationale for assets, asset-building policies, and IDAs for the poor. In R. Boshara (Ed.), *Building Assets: A Report on the Asset-Development and IDA Field* (pp. 2.005-2.024). Washington, D.C.: Corporation for Enterprise Development.

End Notes

[1] Leydorf, D. & Kaplan, D. (May 2001) Use of Individual Development Accounts by people with disabilities: Barriers and solutions. Oakland, CA: World Institute on Disability.

[2] National Organization on Disability/Louis Harris and Associates, Inc. (2000) Employment rates of people with disabilities. National Organization on Disability/Louis Harris and Associates: *2000 Survey of Americans with Disabilities*.

[3] Leydorf & Kaplan, 2001.

[4] Edwards, K. & Mason, L.M. (May 2003) Policy Report: State Policy Trends for Individual Development Accounts in the United States: 1993-2003. St. Louis, MO: Washington University George Warren Brown School of Social Work.

[5] Leydorf & Kaplan, 2001.

[6] Ibid.

[7] Ibid.

[8] Ibid.

[9] Center for Social Development, Washington University George Warren Brown School of Social Work. Available at: http://www.gwbweb.wustl.edu/csd/asset/add.htm

[10] The Downpayments on the American Dream Policy Demonstration (ADD) was supported by 11 foundations including: the Ford Foundation, Charles Stewart Mott Foundation, Joyce Foundation, Citigroup Foundation, F.B. Heron Foundation, John D. and Catherine T. MacArthur Foundation, Fannie Mae Foundation, Levi Strauss Foundation, Ewing Marion Kauffman Foundation, Rockefeller Foundation, and the Moriah Fund.

[11] ADD Partner Sites included (1) Advocap, Inc. in Oshkosh, WI; (2) Alternatives Federal Credit Union in Ithaca, NY; (3) Bay Area IDA Collaborative in Oakland, CA; (4) Capital Area Asset Building Corporation (CAAB) in Washington, D.C.; (5) Community Action Project of Tulsa County (CAPTC) in Tulsa OK; (6) Foundations Communities in Austin, TX; (7) Central Vermont Community Action Council (CVCAC) in Barre, VT; (8) Heart of America Family Focus Center in Kansas City, MO; (9) Mercy Corps in Portland, OR; (10) Owsley County Action Team in Booneville, KY; (11) Near Eastside IDA Program in Indianapolis, IN; (12) Shorebank Corporation in Chicago, IL; and (13) Women's Self-Employment Project in Chicago, IL.

[12] Individual Development Accounts. Retrieved August 5, 2005 from: Center for Social Development, Washington University George Warren Brown School of Social Work. Available at: http://www.gwbweb.wustl.edu/csd/asset/idas.htm

[13] P.L. 105-285.

[14] Ibid.

[15] Ibid.

[16] Ibid.

[17] Ibid.

[18] Boshara, R. (December, 2001) Building Assets: A Report on the Asset-Development and IDA Field. Washington, D.C.: Center for Enterprise Development.

[19] Ibid.

[20] Ibid.

[21] Ibid.

[22] Ibid.

[23] Ibid.

[24] Ibid.

[25] Ibid.

[26] Ibid.

[27] Ibid.

[28] Ibid.

[29] Ibid.

[30] Schreiner, M. (2000). *A Framework for financial benefit-cost analysis of Individual Development Accounts at the experimental site of the Downpayment on the American Dream Policy Demonstration.* St. Louis, MO: Washington University in St. Louis, Center for Social Development. *As quoted in*, Boshara, R., ed. (2001). *Building Assets: A Report on the Asset-Development and IDA Field.* Washington, D.C.: CFED.

[31] Edwards & Mason, 2003.

[32] The section on Iowa is based on information from the Iowans Save! website. Available at: http://www.ised.org/EconomicDevelopment/iowanssave.asp and http://www.ised.org/EconomicDevelopment/ida5year.asp.

[33] Full names are omitted to protect personal privacy.

[34] The average return on EITC investment is $1,500 but some people have received as much as $4,000.

[35] Edwards & Mason, 2003.

[36] Ibid.

[37] Ibid.

In: Creating Livable Communities for People... ISBN: 978-1-60741-534-3
Editor: Alise Vanags

Chapter 6

STRATEGY FIVE: AGREEMENT ON CHANGES IN INFRASTRUCTURE TO CONSOLIDATE ADMINISTRATION OF MULTIPLE PROGRAMS AND IMPROVE EASE OF ACCESS

National Council on Disability

Livable communities provide residents with access to employment opportunities and transportation options. But access to employment and transportation—which are inextricably linked—is among the most vexing barriers that people with disabilities face, partly because of lack of coordination among the various agencies and programs involved. The examples in Strategy Five illustrate how consolidation and coordination can improve access to these key livable community objectives.

WORKFORCE INVESTMENT ACT (WIA)

Congress passed the Workforce Investment Act (WIA) in 1998 to better serve job seekers and employers through a new framework that brings together multiple federal employment and training programs into a unified system of support.[1] The single system is anchored by comprehensive One-Stop centers in each workforce investment area in all fifty states.

Four separate federal agencies—the Departments of Labor, Health and Human Services, Education, and Housing and Urban Development fund 17 categories of programs that provide services through the One-Stop system.[2] The Workforce Investment Act offers one of the most significant attempts to date to reexamine the way services are delivered to individuals in need of public assistance that recognizes the importance of consolidating categorical programs and streamlining service delivery to more efficiently and effectively meet the needs of target populations. Although WIA allows state and local governments the authority to design how best to implement the One-Stop system, the guiding principles of the Act require a focus on streamlined and integrated service with an emphasis on improved coordination and collaboration across agency lines.[3]

More than 80 percent of the state One-Stop Center plans include persons with disabilities and/or representatives of public and private agencies, such as vocational rehabilitation programs, that serve persons with disabilities in the state plan development process.[4]

Grant funds were used to purchase and install assistive and adaptive technologies in Resource Rooms to remove barriers to the use of information technology and to create greater program accessibility. The purchase of equipment was typically accompanied by training and technical assistance with frontline workforce development staff in the One-Stops to improve their understanding of using assistive technology to eliminate barriers to program accessibility.[5]

The majority of projects developed and implemented One-Stop Accessibility Plans that have removed many information technology, physical, and other program barriers. In addition, the majority of projects worked to develop accessibility guidelines for One-Stop Center Staff, and they continue to make accessibility guidelines a focus of activity in the State Workforce Investment Board and Local Workforce Investment Board working groups on disability issues in which they participate. Moreover, several projects developed and used accessibility checklists and survey tools to evaluate current physical and program access of One-Stops and provide assistance to reduce and eliminate barriers.[6]

Partnerships were established to help coordinate services for customers with disabilities in the One-Stop system. A focus of activities was to improve collaboration and resource support between mandated partners and non-mandated partners, including the Social Security Administration's benefits counseling program, Vocational Rehabilitation (VR), Special Education, and Mental Health services.[7]

Multiple strategies were implemented to coordinate with employers regarding opportunities for job seekers with disabilities. Several projects offered seminars and training for employers or developed employer toolkits to educate the business community on the advantages of hiring individuals with disabilities and providing accommodations to employees.[8]

A majority of projects provided education and training on identifying and assisting customers with disabilities to various staff members in One-Stop Centers, including frontline staff, Resource Room staff, and employment counselors. In addition, several projects provided training to employers, as well as to mandated and non-mandated partners.[9]

Multiple strategies were designed and implemented in an effort to market to and reach jobseekers with disabilities, employers, the business community, One-Stop Centers, local boards, the disability community, and youth with disabilities. A majority of projects used marketing and outreach materials, including printed materials (e.g., flyers, brochures, posters, and newspaper and newsletter articles), joint activities with disability agencies, communication with schools, and websites.

Despite past negative impacts on individuals with disabilities under the Job Training Partnership Act, the Workforce Investment Act offers meaningful opportunities for employment and asset development.

Program Background

When the Workforce Investment Act was enacted in 1998, it was a response to continued concerns of multiple stakeholders about the need to change the way employment and training services were delivered. It replaced the Job Training Partnership Act (JTPA) with three new programs—Adult, Dislocated Worker, and Youth. With an intent to make accessing employment and training services easier for job seekers, WIA consolidated 17 categories of programs, totaling over 15 billion dollars from four separate federal agencies into a unified One-Stop service delivery system.[10] The following table identifies the consolidated employment and training programs.

In order for a state to receive WIA funds, it must submit a state plan that describes its approach to the delivery of services through an integrated, seamless service delivery system anchored by comprehensive One-Stop Career Centers.[11] States are provided the option of submitting a Unified Plan to meet Title I State Plan Requirements.[12] A state may submit a Unified Plan that includes Vocational Rehabilitation programs authorized under the Rehabilitation Act (Title IV of WIA), Adult Education and Family Literacy programs, and Title I of WIA incorporating core, intensive, and training services.

Table 4. WIA Mandatory Programs and Their Related Federal Agencies

Federal Agency	Mandatory Program
Department of Labor	WIA Adult
	WIA Dislocated Worker
	WIA Youth
	Employment Service (Wagner-Peyser)
	Trade adjustment assistance programs
	Veterans' employment and training programs
	Unemployment Insurance
	Job Corps
	Welfare-to-Work grant-funded programs
	Senior community service employment program
	Employment and training for migrant and seasonal farm workers
	Employment and training for Native Americans
Department of Education	Vocational Rehabilitation Program
	Adult Education and Literacy
	Vocational Education (Perkins Act)
Department of Health and Human Services	Community Services Block Grant
Department of Housing and Urban Development	HUD-administered employment and training

The guidance to states from the Employment and Training Administration of the U.S. Department of Labor defines national strategic directions including but not limited to: Integrated, seamless service delivery through comprehensive One-Stop Career Centers; maximum flexibility in tailoring service delivery and making strategic investment in workforce development activities to meet the need of state and local economies and labor markets; customers making informed choices based on quality training providers and increased fiscal and performance accountability.[13]

The intent of this unified planning is to encourage states to design and implement an integrated service delivery system that reduces overlap or duplication among programs and established policies and procedures and ensures collaboration among partner agencies. States are required to describe in their Unified Plan innovative service delivery strategies the state has or is planning to undertake to maximize resources, increase service levels, improve service quality, and achieve better integration.[14] A state is required to describe its strategies to ensure that the full range of employment and training programs and services delivered through the One-Stop system are accessible and meet the needs of people with disabilities. With respect to the Vocational Rehabilitation program, a state must describe in a Unified Plan application what policies and procedures will be put in place to improve coordination and non-duplication of services with other public and private non-profit agencies or organizations.

Program Description

Under Title I of the Workforce Investment Act (WIA), each state's governor is required to establish a State Workforce Investment Board, designate local workforce investment areas, and oversee the creation of local Workforce Investment Boards and the network of One-Stop Centers statewide.[15] The One-Stop system is the basic delivery mechanism for adult and dislocated worker services. Services are organized into three levels: core, intensive, and training services. In addition, supportive services may be provided to individuals who are participating in core, intensive, or training services so that the services are effective and meaningful.[16]

Core services must be made available on a universal basis to individuals 18 years old or older. WIA regulations identify 11 categories of core services including initial assessment, job search, placement and career counseling information and referral to supportive services, and follow-up on services.[17] Job seekers in need of additional assistance may be eligible for intensive services. Intensive service may include development of an individual employment plan, individual and group counseling, case management, and short-term pre-vocational services.[18] As a result of more comprehensive and specialized assessment of skill levels and service needs, a job seeker may be identified as a candidate for training services that include occupational skills training, skills upgrading and retraining, adult literacy, and customized training with a commitment to hire the individual on completion of the training.[19] In the event that WIA funds allocated to a local workforce investment area are limited, priority must be given to recipients of public assistance and other low-income individuals for intensive training services.

The One-Stops are the anchor of the workforce delivery system. Each workforce investment area designated by a state's governor must include at least one comprehensive physical center in each local area that must provide access to other programs and activities carried out by One-Stop partners.[20] Each of the mandated partners must enter into a memorandum of understanding (MOU) with the local Workforce Investment Board (WIB) to describe roles and responsibilities, the service to be provided, and methods of referral and coordination. A single umbrella MOU may be developed between the Local Board and all partners, or the partners may decide to enter into separate agreements between the Board and one or more partners.[21]

All states and local workforce investment areas must report regularly to the U.S. Department of Labor based on four core indicators of performance. For the adult program, these indicators are a) entry into unsubsidized employment, b) retention in unsubsidized employment six months after entry into employment, c) earning level six months after entry into employment, and d) attainment of recognized credentials related to achievement of educational skills by participants who entered unsubsidized employment.[22]

Lessons Learned

It has been six years since states began implementation of Title I of WIA (July 2000). Two GAO Reports in June 2003 and December 2004 examined One-Stop strategies to strengthen service and partnerships and access and participation for persons with disabilities.[23] In the first study, GAO visited 14 One-Stop Centers nationwide to learn more about current activities to consolidate programs, strengthen program partnerships, and streamline service delivery for job seekers. All of the centers visited used at least one of three different strategies to build a more streamlined system that improves access to services, provides more knowledgeable staff about the full range of service options available through partner agencies, and consolidates case management and intake procedures. Co-location of staff, cross-training of staff, and coordinated planning meetings to identify and access resources to overcome barriers to employment for individual job seekers were all strategies identified by GAO as improvements to service delivery. GAO did identify that current tracking of individual outcome data did not provide information about the impact of various One-Stop integrated service delivery approaches.

The second GAO study focused exclusively on access to One-Stops for persons with disabilities. The focus of inquiry extended beyond access questions to examine the various relationships between the One-Stops and other disability-related agencies providing services to persons with disabilities. GAO visited 10 local areas and One-Stops nationwide. The Department of Labor has awarded over 100 grants and 80 million dollars in the last four years for disability-related activities to enhance access and meaningful participation of persons with disabilities in the workforce development system. In addition to these capacity building grants, all One-Stops must comply with Section 188 of WIA to:

- Take steps to ensure that communications with individuals with disabilities are as effective as communications with others, including providing appropriate auxiliary aids and services where necessary;
- Provide reasonable accommodation to qualified individuals with disabilities who are applicants, registrants, or eligible applicants/ registrants for, or participants in, employers of, or applicants for, employment with their programs and activities, unless providing the accommodation would cause undue hardship;
- Make reasonable modification in policies, practices, or procedures, unless making the modifications would fundamentally alter the nature of the service, program, or activity;
- Provide the most integrated setting appropriate to the needs of qualified individuals with disabilities; and
- Take appropriate steps, such as advertising and marketing, to ensure that they are providing universal access to their WIA financially assisted programs and activities.

The GAO report concluded that the local areas and One-Stops visited had made varying degrees of progress in improving physical and communication access. However, a number of the One-Stops were still automatically referring all persons with disabilities to VR, and there were limited relationships developed with other disability service providers and funders. GAO's concluding recommendations urge the Department of Labor to develop a long-term plan to improve access to a seamless, comprehensive service delivery system that leverages and coordinates resources more effectively.

Conclusion

The Workforce Investment Act provides a framework to consolidate federally funded programs with similar goals and objectives. The potential for a streamlined service delivery system with improved access for jobseekers with and without disabilities remains viable as states and local workforce investment areas continue to improve partner agency relationships, improve awareness and understanding of specific agency resources, and establish policies, procedures, and structures to be responsive to customer needs and expectations.

A seamless system of universal access, common application for services, cross-agency staff training, planning, and collaborative case management and resource sharing are all important ingredients in making a community more livable for people with disabilities.

Resources

Workforce Investment Act: One-Stop Centers Implemented Strategies to Strengthen Services and Partnerships, but More Research and Information Sharing is Needed. GAO-03-725 http://www.gao.gov/new.items/d03725.pdf

Workforce Investment Act: States and Local Areas Have Developed Strategies to Assess Performance, but Labor Could Do More to Help. GAO-04-657 http://www.gao.gov/new.items/d04657.pdf

Workforce Investment Act: Labor Has Taken Several Actions to Facilitate Access to One-Stops for Persons with Disabilities, but These Efforts May Not Be Sufficient. GAO-05-54, http://www.gao.gov/new.items/d0554.pdf

"A Description of the Workforce Investment Act Legal Framework from a Disability Policy Perspective" - Bobby Silverstein http://disability.law.uiowa.edu/lhpdc/rrtc/documents/silverstein/WIA_full.doc

"A Preliminary Analysis of the Relationship between the Workforce Investment Act and the Federal Disability Policy Framework" - Bobby Silverstein http://disability.law.uiowa.edu/lhpdc/rrtc/documents/silverstein/WIA_PRE_full.doc

WIA Information and Tools http://www.doleta.gov/usworkforce/wia/

UNITED WE RIDE: LEARNING FROM AND HELPING THE STATES TO CREATE COORDINATED TRANSPORTATION SYSTEMS

Program Description

The need for *consolidation* and *coordination* is keenly felt by the states in the area of transportation. In 2003, the Government Accountability Office (GAO) issued a report on "transportation disadvantaged populations" that identified 62 different federal programs across 8 federal agencies that provide funding that may be used for community transportation services for people with disabilities, persons with lower incomes, and older adults. The report also noted that there are multiple public and private agencies that provide human service transportation[24] in any one community, and services vary greatly in terms of eligibility requirements, hours or scope of operation, specific destinations, and quality. Given the multiplicity of programs and the significant dollar amounts spent, more effective coordination is needed to ensure better service to more people, particularly when federal, state, and local budgets for human service activities are under extreme pressure.

In 2004, President Bush signed Executive Order 13330 to establish the Interagency Transportation Coordinating Council on Access and Mobility (CCAM) to improve coordination among these various transportation programs. The Council is composed of 11 federal departments (i.e., Departments of Transportation, Health and Human Services, Labor, Education, Housing and Urban Development, Agriculture, Justice, and the Interior; as well as the Veterans' Administration, the Social Security Administration, and the National Council on Disability).

In 2005, the CCAM submitted a report to the President outlining several recommendations that the Council believes will strengthen existing transportation services and make them more cost-effective, accountable, and responsive to consumers. These recommendations and the related action plan to implement the executive order focus on:

- Education and outreach to transportation providers in order to encourage and facilitate coordination, and to consumers to help them access the most appropriate transportation service for their needs; the development of a central website for information management and materials for human service transportation coordination

- Consolidation of programs to simplify access to transportation services and enhance customer service; tools to help people navigate and use all the service options available, such as transit passes, vouchers, and travel training; and computerized, consolidated reservation, scheduling, dispatch, payment, billing, and reporting systems
- Reduction of restrictive and duplicative laws, regulations, and programs related to human service transportation at the federal level, including duplication and conflict among statutes and regulations across the 62 federal programs; consideration and implementation of waiver demonstration programs
- Coordinated planning, including a "Framework for Action" developed for and implemented in states; documentation of the current status of human services transportation coordination; and joint planning demonstration projects at the state and community levels
- Cost allocation methodology and guidance to be developed and implemented
- Documentation of successful strategies in coordinating human service transportation at the federal, state, tribal, and local levels

The United We Ride program is cataloging "useful practices" and providing technical assistance and training to the states as well as opportunities for states to submit proposals for grants to develop and implement comprehensive state action plans for coordinating human service transportation. Grants under this initiative range from $35,000 to $75,000. In 2004, 45 states received United We Ride State Coordination grants and a new round of grants was awarded in 2005 to states that propose to address one of the following priorities: 1) development and implementation of transit pass policy and programs with Medicaid and other agencies; 2) development of strategies for meeting the transportation needs of older adults, people with disabilities, and individuals with lower incomes during natural or man-made disasters; and 3) development of a cross-agency coordinated tracking and accountability systems; including real time eligibility, billing, and reporting.

Arizona Rides

Arizona is one of United We Ride's first grantees. Soon after President Bush's Executive Order was issued in 2004, the governor of Arizona, Janet

Napolitano, called for a working group to begin building a human services transportation strategy for the state. In 2004, the working group submitted a grant proposal to assist with this planning, and the United We Ride grant was awarded in 2005. In 2005, lending further commitment to improved transportation coordination in Arizona, the Governor signed an executive order formalizing an "Arizona Rides" initiative and instituting the Arizona Rides Council, with membership including the Arizona Department of Health Services, Arizona Department of Economic Security, Arizona Health Care Cost Containment System, Arizona Department of Corrections, Arizona Council of Governments, Governor's Office of Highway Safety, Governor's Office of Intergovernmental Affairs, and others.

The express purpose of the Arizona Rides initiative is to provide assistance to Arizona local governments and human service agencies in coordinating human services transportation. In her executive order, the Governor asserted that Arizona has a strong commitment to providing public transportation to persons with disabilities, older adults, and low-income families and individuals. She charged the Arizona Rides Council to develop a statewide coordination action plan and conduct related activities to 1) establish relationships between state, federal, and local entities to achieve a coordinated approach to human services transportation in the state; 2) build knowledge of successful approaches to coordinated human services transportation that can be used to promote such coordination in Arizona communities; and 3) increase communication and collaboration between state agencies in order to efficiently disseminate federal transportation and human services funds.

Arizona Rides retained a consulting firm to conduct a statewide assessment of the current human services transportation system. This Statewide Assessment of Human Service Transportation Project is developing an inventory of providers, consumers, funding sources, service characteristics, and transportation opportunities and barriers. In addition, the study will identify areas where federal transportation reimbursement and grants can be obtained. This project is working in conjunction with a pilot coordination project among transportation providers in the Pinal County area in Central Arizona, an historically rural area that is experiencing rapid urban growth. The goal of this pilot project is to develop coordination tools that other regions in the state could use in their own communities.

Arizona Rides is still in the "discovery phase," trying to understand what the current transportation situation is before developing its implementation plan. For more information on this program and to follow its progress, see http://www.azdot.gov/PTD/UnitedWeRide.asp

Other State Transportation Coordination Efforts

The United We Ride initiative is relatively new, but various states have been working on transportation coordination for many years. To recognize these efforts, United We Ride instituted the Leadership Awards Program and presented awards to 10 communities that have developed exemplary models of transportation coordination.

Winners of the awards include the following:

North Carolina

In North Carolina, a 1978 Executive Order mandated coordination of transportation resources and established a state-interagency North Carolina Human Service Transportation Council (HSTC) that provides policy recommendations to the Department of Health and Human Services (DHHS), Department of Transportation (DOT), and other state agencies in addressing needs, barriers, and opportunities for the provision of human service transportation. There is long-established communication and collaboration on human service transportation issues between the North Carolina DOT and the North Carolina DHHS. As a result, a full-time departmental level Transportation Program Administrator position was established within DHHS that is fully funded by DOT.

North Carolina was the first state in the nation to require a Transportation Memorandum of Understanding at the local level that assures coordination between the transportation system and humans service agencies. In order to be eligible for Community Transportation Program funds, DOT requires each local transportation system to have a transportation advisory or governing board, which includes representation from the local Department of Social Services, the Aging Program, the Public Health Department, Mental Health and Community Rehabilitative Facilities, and the local Center for Independent Living on the transportation advisory board/governing board to ensure that public transportation services continue to meet the needs of individuals with disabilities.

As a result of these collaborative efforts, all 100 North Carolina counties have human service transportation systems to serve the transportation disadvantaged. Additionally, the state has established a web-based "Cross County Transit Project" that allows users to coordinate non-emergency medical transportation trips across county jurisdiction lines to regional health care facilities. The state is currently working on establishing recommendations for uniform transportation reporting requirements for human service transportation service programs.

Maryland

Maryland's 1997 Executive Order established the Maryland Coordinating Committee for Human Services Transportation and launched the state's effort in addressing transportation coordination with human services agencies. The committee, chaired by the Maryland Transit Administration (MTA), represents a cross-section of human service and employment agencies. A five-year human services transportation plan was approved by the state agencies represented on the Committee to provide a foundation for improved coordination of services and funds to help the state meet current and growing mobility needs. To give guidance and recommendations to Maryland's human service transportation providers, the MTA developed a comprehensive Maryland Transportation Coordination Manual.

The Maryland Job Access and Reverse Commute Program, which relies heavily on partnerships, has become a national model of coordination, providing over three million rides since its inception.

ACCESS Transportation Systems, sponsored by Port Authority of Allegheny County, is one of the largest coordinated paratransit programs (transportation services required by the Americans with Disabilities Act for people unable to use fixed-route transportation like buses and taxis) in the nation, providing about 1.9 million rides annually primarily to individuals with disabilities, those with low incomes, and older adults. About 35% of ACCESS's trips are sponsored by more than 125 participating agencies that purchase transportation services. A founding principle of the ACCESS program in 1979 was coordination, which was seen as a way to avoid costly duplication of service, thereby making the maximum dollars available for the highest quality, least restricted service possible.

Thanks to coordination of combined resources with its partners, ACCESS is a strong and extensive system, serving all of Allegheny County seven days per week, 365 days per year, 6 a.m. to midnight. There are 430 vehicles in use on an average weekday, with assistance provided through the door, including assistance up or down up to four steps. The system design is a reflection of the community's commitment to a transportation system that provides full mobility for its users.

Central New York, NY

The Central New York Regional Transportation Authority (CNYRTA) is a public authority and a public benefit corporation of New York State, created in 1970. Its purpose is to continue, further develop, and improve transportation and related services in the Central New York Transportation District. Of the seven New York counties eligible to join the transportation district, three counties have been part of the authority district since at least 1973 and a fourth commenced service on April 1, 2005. CNYRTA provides approximately 12 million passenger trips annually, covering more than 5.2 million miles of service with a combined fleet of 208 small and large buses.

Examples of CNYRTA's efforts to implement new, innovative strategies to improve the coordination of public and human services transportation include coordinating ride services with the paratransit division and several local not-for-profit agencies in 1978; enhancing transportation services for foster families/grandchildren; access to nutrition, shopping centers, and medical care for seniors; and improved access to employment opportunities for visually impaired individuals. In 1985, CNYRTA expanded to include the Metropolitan Commission on Aging, increasing the availability of coordinated services to the area's senior population. Medicaid transportation was added in 1996, providing enhanced transportation alternatives for Medicaid patients traveling to and from their doctor/hospital appointments. Projects in 1999 addressed the growing needs of low-income individuals/families by leveraging Temporary Assistance for Needy Families (TANF) Job Access and Reverse Commute (JARC) funding.

CNYRTA was one of the first transportation providers in the state to form partnerships with local employers, colleges, universities, and other community sectors when it implemented its Mobility Management Center (MMC) in 1999 and today is a one-stop transportation center. Other unique aspects of this system are that it provides individualized trip planning, directing individuals to lower cost fixed-route services; computer assistance scheduling/dispatching software; automated passenger counters; and automated vehicle location to aid development and implementation of coordinated transportation services.

For more information about United We Ride, these and other winners of the Leadership Awards Program, and "useful practices" implemented by states and counties, see http://www.unitedweride.gov.

End Notes

[1] Public Law 105-220.

[2] GAO, Workforce Investment Act: States and Local Areas have Developed Strategies to Asses Performance, but Labor Could Do More To Help (Washington, DC – June 1, 2004).

[3] 64 FR 9403-9404 (February 25, 1999).

[4] University of Iowa, Law, Health Policy & Disability Center, *Review of State Plans for the Workforce Investment Act From a Disability Policy Framework: Executive Summary*, Michael Morris and Bobby Silverstein, p. vii. Available at: http://disability.law.uiowa.edu/lhpdc/rrtc/documents/morris/WIA_Executive_Summary.doc

[5] WIG Process Evaluation And Navigator Supplemental Survey Analysis, Round Three Grantees, Year 1. Document produced by the Law, Health Policy & Disability Center (LHPDC), University of Iowa College of Law. Document produced for the Division of Disability and Workforce Programs, Employment and Training Administration.

[6] Ibid.

[7] Ibid.

[8] Ibid.

[9] Ibid.

[10] GAO, Workforce Investment Act: One-Stop Centers Implemented Strategies to Strengthen Services and Partnerships, but More Research and Information Sharing Is Needed (Washington, DC – June 18, 2003).

[11] 64 FR 9406 (February 25, 1999).

[12] Section 501 of WIA (29 U.S.C. 2832).

[13] 20 CFR 661.400(b) (February 25, 1999).

[14] 65 FR 2477 (January 14, 2000).

[15] Section 117 of WIA (29 U.S.C. 2832).

[16] 20 CFR 662.100(a).

[17] 20 CFR 662.240.

[18] 134 (d)(3)(c) of WIA and 20 CFR 663.200.

[19] 134 (d)(4)(d) of WIA and 20 CFR 663.300.

[20] 134 (c)(2) of WIA and 20 CFR 662.100(d).

[21] 20 CFR 662.310(a).

[22] 20CFR 666.100.

[23] GAO, Workforce Investment Act: Labor Has Taken Several Actions to Facilitate Access to One-Stops For Persons With Disabilities, But These Efforts May Not Be Sufficient (Washington, DC – December 14, 2004).

[24] Human service transportation includes a broad range of transportation service options designed to meet the needs of "transportation disadvantaged" populations, including older adults, disabled persons, and/or those with lower incomes.

In: Creating Livable Communities for People... ISBN: 978-1-60741-534-3
Editor: Alise Vanags

Chapter 7

STRATEGY SIX: UTILIZATION OF WAIVER AUTHORITY TO PROMOTE STATE OPTIONS TO ADVANCE CONSUMER CHOICE AND COMMUNITY PARTICIPATION

National Council on Disability

The primary objective of the livable community concept is to provide people with disabilities choice and support to live independently in the community. The examples in Strategy Six illustrate long-term services and supports policies that support this objective. Many people believe that long-term services and supports alternatives like state Medicaid waiver programs should be the rule rather than the exception.

MEDICAID AND SOCIAL SECURITY WAIVER AUTHORITY

Medicaid and Social Security offer two important sources of funding for support of individuals with disabilities. Medicaid offers states the opportunity to receive federal financial assistance to share in the cost of a wide range of community services. Individual states have some flexibility in the determination of eligibility and the scope of services covered. When first enacted as Title XIX of the Social Security Act in 1965, Medicaid was intended to provide a limited federal entitlement to purchase acute health care for low-income individuals and families.[1] Over the past 25 years, significant expansion of Medicaid has occurred through the creation of waiver authority. Waiver authority allows states to apply to the federal Centers for Medicare and Medicaid Services (CMS) for approval of different amendments to their state plans that may impact who is eligible for services, what services may be covered, and the limits of coverage.

Similarly, the Social Security Administration (SSA) has waiver authority it can grant to states on a case-by-case basis to modify existing policies and procedures and encourage testing alternative policies and procedures that promote independence and self-sufficiency for individuals with disabilities and their families.

Medicaid Program Background

Medicaid is an entitlement program designed to help states meet the costs of medically necessary health care for low-income and medically needy populations. When first enacted, Medicaid mandated coverage of primary and acute health care services and included limited long-term services and supports coverage in skilled nursing facilities for individuals aged 21 years and older. States are required to cover certain populations and provide fourteen basic mandatory services to all eligible, needy groups.[2] The federal Medicaid requirements prohibit states from placing limits on mandated services solely because of diagnosis, type of illness, or condition. States must specify the amount, duration, and scope for each service they provide, which must be sufficient to reasonably achieve its purposes.[3]

Beyond the federally required mandatory services, a state may elect to include other optional benefits in its program. A state has more flexibility in defining the specific services it offers within an optional service category. Table 5 lists Mandatory Medicaid benefits and Optional Medicaid Services.

In response to the increasingly higher costs of nursing facility care and the institutional bias which was part of the initial authority in 1970, home health services became a mandatory benefit.[4] In 1981, Congress authorized the Home and Community Based Services (HCBS) waiver authority.[5] The 1915(c) waiver, named after the section of the Social Security Act that authorized it, allows states to provide services not usually covered by the Medicaid program to keep a person from being institutionalized. Home- and community-based services (other than room and board) for specific eligible populations are now part of waiver programs in all 50 states.

Table 5. Mandatory Medicaid Benefits and Optional Medicaid Services

Mandatory Medicaid Benefits	
• Inpatient hospital services • Outpatient hospital services • Prenatal care • Physician services • Nursing facility services for persons age 21 or older • Home health services • Federally qualified health-center (FQHC) services, and FQHC ambulatory services otherwise covered by Medicaid in other settings	• Rural health clinic services • Laboratory and x-ray services • Nurse-midwife services • Vaccines for children • Family planning services and supplies • Pediatric and family nurse practitioner services • Early and periodic screening, diagnostic, and treatment (EPSDT) services for children under age 21
Optional Services	
• Diagnostic services • Clinic services • Intermediate care facilities for the mentally retarded (ICFs/MR) • Nursing facility services for children under age 21 • Rehabilitative services • Physical and occupational therapy • Speech pathology and audiology services • Dental services and dentures • Inpatient mental health services for individuals age 65 and older • Hospice care • Case management • Other medical or remedial care furnished by licensed practitioners under state law • Durable medical equipment • Transportation services	• Optometrist services and eyeglasses • Home and community-based services as an alternative to institutionalization • Prescribed drug and prosthetic devices • Chiropractic services • Private duty nursing services • Screening and preventative service • TB-related services for TB infected individuals • Inpatient psychiatric facility for people under age 22 • Program of All-inclusive Care for the Elderly (PACE) • Personal care/assistance • Respiratory care for ventilator-dependent individuals • Prosthetic devices

In addition to the HCBS waiver authority, there is also a Section 1115 waiver authority. Section 1115 of the Social Security Act provides CMS broad authority to support experimental, pilot, or demonstration projects to test new ideas related to the financing and delivery of medical and supportive services. The proposed experiment or demonstration must be a program model that had not been tested previously and could not be conducted within the boundaries of a more limited waiver authority, such as the HCBS waiver. A Section 1115 waiver must be budget neutral over the life of a project, typically five years. In other words, the model cannot be expected to cost the Federal Government more than it would cost without the waiver. There are a number of states with current 1115 demonstration projects that are testing managed-care approaches covering acute and long-term services. Other states are using 1115 authority to test self-directed support plans, individual budgets, and the hiring of family members to provide services.[6]

Program Description

States may offer a variety of services to participants under an HCBS waiver program and are not limited to the number of services that can be provided. For an individual to be eligible under a specific HCBS waiver, the individual must meet targeting and service criteria. Targeting criteria may involve age, diagnosis, or condition. Most states have multiple waivers targeted to different groups, such as persons with traumatic brain injury, persons with AIDS, and persons with intellectual and developmental disabilities.

Individuals who meet the targeting criteria must then meet the service criteria, which usually requires the individual to meet the eligibility requirements to enter either a hospital or nursing facility or Intermediate Care Facility for persons with intellectual, and the defined home- and community-based services to be provided have to correspond to the level of care provided in institutional settings. States must demonstrate that waiver services are only being provided to individuals who are eligible for institutional placement. Equivalent criteria for waiver services and for institutional placement stem from the waiver program's primary purpose, which is to offer alternatives to institutional placement.[7]

States have the flexibility to design an HCBS waiver to meet the specific needs of defined groups. HCBS can be divided into five overarching categories: personal care and assistance; specialty services, including access to assistive technology; adaptive services, including home and vehicle modifications; family and caregiver supports, including respite care; and social supports and case management or service coordination.[8]

States may use an HCBS waiver to provide a combination of both traditional medical services (i.e. dental services, speech and occupational therapy) as well as non-medical services (respite care, environmental modifications, and service coordination). There is no limit on the number of services that can be offered under a single waiver program as long as the waiver retains cost-neutrality and the services are necessary to avoid institutionalization. Two important requirements of mandatory and optional services coverage under a state's Medicaid plan are not required under an HCBS waiver. Under a "comparability requirement," a state cannot offer a mandatory or optional service only to persons who have a particular condition or offer it in different forms to different groups.[9] Under the "statewideness requirement," a state cannot offer a mandatory or optional service to a particular geographic region.[10] With federal approval, however, a state can design an HCBS waiver that waives both the comparability and statewideness requirements so that services are targeted to a specific number of individuals in a defined group and in only one area or region of the state. A state may choose to cover a specific service such as personal assistance services at a basic level in its state plan, and then build on this level of coverage through waiver programs to provide additional support to specific target populations.

Independence Plus Waivers

On May 9, 2002, Secretary Tommy Thompson, who was Secretary of the Department of Health and Human Services (DHHS) at the time, unveiled the *Independence Plus* initiative in response to Executive Order 13217, in which DHHS promised to provide states with simplified model waiver and demonstration application templates that would promote person-centered planning and self-directed service options.[11]

Independence Plus is based on the experiences and lessons learned from states that pioneered consumer self-direction. Specifically, two national pilot projects demonstrated the success of these approaches in the 1990s: (a) the Self-Determination project in 19 states that focused primarily on the Home- and Community-Based Services §1915(c) waivers, and (b) the "Cash and Counseling" project in 3 states that focused on the §1115 demonstrations. These programs allowed service recipients or their families the option to direct the design and delivery of services and supports they received, with the goals of avoiding unnecessary institutionalization, experiencing higher levels of satisfaction, and maximizing the efficient use of community services and supports.[12]

The §1915(c) and §1115 Demonstration Applications have different approaches and distinctly different authorizing provisions of the Social Security Act. The following table compares the two application approaches[13]:

Table 6. Section 1115 Demonstration Authority vs. Section 1915(c) HCBS Waiver Authority

Issue	Section 1115 Demonstration Authority	Section 1915(c) HCBS Waiver Authority
Cash allowance	Participants may manage the cash allowance directly	Participant does not manage cash allowance directly
Hiring legally responsible individuals	States may hire legally responsible individuals	States may hire legally responsible individuals
Provider agreements	Provider agreements may be waived	Provider agreements must be executed
Direct payments to providers	Direct payments by the Medicaid agency to providers may be waived	Direct payments by the Medicaid agency to providers may be waived
Payment for services made prior to delivery of services	Services may be reimbursed prior to delivery	Services must be delivered prior to payment
Level of care	Level of care may vary	Individuals meet institutional level of care
Services which may be self-directed (presents participants with the option to control and direct Medicaid funds identified in an Individual Budget).	State plan of HCBS services	HCBS services only
Combining populations	States may combine any population	Combining populations is limited by: age/disability, intellectual disability/developmental disability, mental illness, or any subgroup thereof

CMS is consolidating the existing *Independence Plus* template into a new web-based Section 1915(c) application with instructions. The consolidation enables the expansion of a variety of self-directed options in existing waivers; consistent participant protections across all waiver programs; minimal administrative burden to states; an easier waiver amendment process; and improved communication of expectations for quality.[14]

There are 11 approved *Independence Plus* waivers in 10 states, and several states are working with CMS to submit proposals.[15]

Conclusion

States currently operate over 250 distinct waiver programs.[16] In waiver programs states have the ability to design programs that meet the unique needs of individuals with disabilities. The waiver program is the fastest growing segment of Medicaid, with expenditures and number of persons covered increasing annually by more than 10 percent.[17]

These waiver programs constitute the principal way that states can offer services and supports that are consumer-centered and promote independence and community participation among people with disabilities. There continues to be strong opposition to the inherent institutional bias of Medicaid, as well as support for converting the waiver authority into the main program framework rather than the exception to current Medicaid policy. At the time of writing this report, in the Deficit Reduction Act of 2005 new options were included for states to establish Home- and Community-Based Services as a state plan option without tying back eligibility to an institutional level of care. CMS in 2006 will be issuing program guidance to provide a more detailed explanation for states on design and implementation.[18]

Resources

Schneider, A., Elisa, R., Garfield, R., et al. (2002). *The Medicaid Resource Book.* Menlo Park, CA: The Kaiser Commission on Medicaid and the Uninsured. Available at: http://www.kff.org/medicaid/2236-index.cfm .

Understanding Medicaid Home and Community Based Services: A Primer (2000). Washington DC: Office of the Assistant Secretary for Planning and Evaluation.

Centers for Medicare and Medicaid Services http://cms.hhs.gov/medicaid

State Medicaid Agency Websites http://www.cms.gov/medicaid/allState Contacts.asp

Using Medicaid *to Support Working Age Adults with Serious Mental Illnesses in the Community: A Handbook* (2005). Washington DC: Office of the Assistant Secretary for Planning and Evaluation.

Home and Community-Based Services: Medicaid Research and Demonstration Waivers http://www.pascenter.org/demo_waivers

Centers for Medicare and Medicaid Services Waiver Application and Technical Guide http://www.cms.hhs.gov/medicaid/waivers/quality.asp

Livable Communities for Adults with Disabilities, (2004). Washington, DC: National Council on Disability. Available at: http://www.ncd.gov/newsroom/publications/2004/LivableCommunities.htm

Learning from the States

Implementing the 1915(c) Waiver through Maryland's New Directions Program

Maryland and Florida are profiled here because of their innovative use of Medicaid waiver authority. Maryland is an example of a state that is using the *Independence Plus* initiative of the 1915(c) HCBS waiver program to promote livable community principles, enabling individuals with disabilities to remain in their own homes and communities.

Maryland's New Directions Waiver is a pilot program approved by the Federal Government to allow people receiving services from the Maryland Developmental Disabilities Administration (DDA) to self-direct their services. New Directions is available to people in all parts of the state who are living in their own homes with their families.[19] The program began on July 1, 2005, and during its first year will allow up to 100 people to direct their own services.[20] Individuals who are interested in taking more of a management role in organizing the services they receive are good candidates for this program.

Everyone in New Directions receives an individual budget. With assistance from a Fiscal Management Service (FMS) and a person called a Support Broker, the individual manages his/her budget, hires and supervises his/her own staff, and makes decisions about how the services are provided. The FMS pays bills, takes care of tax paperwork, and provides monthly budget statements. The Support Broker is someone the care recipient trusts to help him/her navigate the system, manage service providers, and act as an advocate on the care recipient's behalf.

Each person enrolled in New Directions develops a plan, with input from family, friends, and others invited to participate, that spells out how the person wants to live his/her life. The plan is the foundation for developing an individual budget, which identifies available funds for approved services.[21]

The New Directions Waiver is designed to increase flexibility and choice for people receiving community supports.[22] Self-Directed Services that are available under New Directions include:

- Assistive technology and adaptive equipment (e.g. communication devices)
- Accessibility adaptations (e.g. grab bars, doors widened, etc.)
- Respite
- Supports brokerage
- Support services
- Supported employment
- Transportation

The following traditional services may be part of the plan, too:[23]

- Behavioral supports
- Resource coordination
- Traditional day services
- Transition services

The Support Broker must:

- Have a criminal background check
- Be trained on person-specific information
- Be familiar with self-directed services and the DDA service system

The Support Broker helps to:

- Develop the plan
- Develop and manage the budget
- Develop an emergency back-up plan
- Manage the services

- Recruit, hire, and supervise the staff

Resource Coordinators are involved with care recipients from the moment planning begins and adjust their level of involvement in response to the amount of help that the care recipients want or need. The Resource Coordinator assists the person in prioritizing what services they need, and will help in the budget development process. The budget is based upon the individual plan.

The Resource Coordinator monitors the individual plan to make sure that services provided are helping to achieve the outcomes identified in the plan. The Resource Coordinator may also check in periodically to make sure that the care recipient is happy with his/her services, including his/her Support Broker. If necessary, the Resource Coordinator reports areas of concern to the Maryland DDA. If all of a care recipient's budget is not spent, the Maryland DDA retains one half of the savings and allows the care recipient to purchase an item in the plan that may not have been originally included in the budget with the remainder of the savings.

The Florida Freedom Initiative: Self-Directed Services with a Work Incentive Plan

The Florida Freedom Initiative (FFI) is an attempt to build on the success of the ongoing "Cash and Counseling" demonstration, called Consumer Directed Care Plus. Florida has been conducting this program with partners that include the Centers for Medicare and Medicaid Services (CMS); the Office of the Assistant Secretary for Planning and Evaluation at the Department of Health and Human Services (DHHS); the National Program Office at the University of Maryland Center on Aging; the Robert Wood Johnson Foundation; the National Council on Aging; and Mathematica Policy Research (as the evaluator).

FFI is an initiative that can be replicated in other states as a way of ensuring that people with disabilities have affordable, accessible services and housing. It is a demonstration being conducted by the Florida Agency for People with Disabilities (formerly the Florida Department of Children and Families) with a grant from CMS. Those who will participate in the demonstration are Medicaid beneficiaries, most of whom have developmental disabilities and use long-term care supports, including the services of a personal attendant. The FFI will test ways to better enable these individuals to live and work in their communities.

Instead of agency-furnished services, FFI participants receive a cash allowance that is set aside in a restricted account. Within certain parameters, participants are able to direct disbursements from the account to purchase supports and services of their choosing to meet their long-term care needs.

The FFI will also promote generation of personal income through work, especially through the development of very small businesses called micro-enterprises. Participants and their support network will receive training in micro-enterprise development.

In conjunction with the FFI, the Social Security Administration (SSA) is conducting a demonstration called Work Incentives for Participants in the Florida Freedom Initiative. The SSA demonstration will provide the following waivers of SSI program rules for FFI participants:

- As in the cash and counseling demonstration, funds received as a cash allowance but not spent will not count as resources during the demonstration, and interest earned by such funds will not count as income
- SSI rules regarding federally supported individual development accounts (IDAs) will apply to non-federally supported IDAs, subject to approval of the IDA program's rules by SSA's Office of Disability and Income Security Programs
- The earned-income exclusion will be $280 plus half the remainder of funds received as cash-allowance, but not spent, instead of $65 plus half the remainder of cash-allowance not spent. The general exclusion of $20 will continue to apply

An individual may specify post-secondary education as the goal of a plan for achieving self-support, or PASS, as long as the plan includes a step for the specification of a work goal at least one year prior to completion of course requirements. A PASS approved with a goal of post-secondary education need not be completed before the Florida Freedom Initiative ends.

SSI beneficiaries participating in the Florida Freedom Initiative will be exempt from continuing disability reviews (CDRs) during the demonstration.

The FFI plans to enroll about 1,100 SSI beneficiaries statewide. Start-up activities began in February 2004. Recently, the Agency for Persons with Disabilities (APD) announced that approximately 6,600 additional persons with developmental disabilities would be served in the 2005–2006 fiscal year

(FY). Letters are already going to individuals on the waitlist to begin the enrollment process.[24] To date, over 3,000 new people have been enrolled for services and supports. Florida's Governor, Jeb Bush, signed the FY2005–2006 State budget that provides the APD with over $1.2 billion to provide services for Floridians with developmental disabilities.[25]

The APD has been able to provide critical services and supports for persons with developmental disabilities to reach their full potential in the home and community. The budget has been increased by 144 percent and in FY2004–2005 served over 33,000 Floridians with developmental disabilities. APD will reach approximately 40,000 persons with developmental disabilities this year, an increase of 18 percent.[26]

California's Independence Plus Section 1115 Demonstration

California's *Independence Plus* Program is called California In-Home Supportive Services (IHSS) Plus Demonstration. California submitted an initial proposal for the program on May 4, 2004, and the proposal was approved by CMS on July 30, 2004. The demonstration program was implemented on August 1, 2004, and is scheduled to expire on July 31, 2009.[27]

The purpose of the program is to provide aged, blind, and disabled adults and children with self-directed personal care assistance and service delivery options. These services and options were previously available under the "Residual Program" (RP) of the IHSS program that has been operating since 1973. The RP was set to be eliminated from the State's budget effective July 1, 2004, however California sought to preserve these self-directed services and options through the Section 1115 authority of the SSA. These services and options have enabled participants to remain in their family residences or in their own homes and helped to avert the need for higher cost institutional care, acute hospital services, and emergency room visits.[28]

The target population includes approximately 66,000 Medi-Cal eligible elders and persons of all ages with disabilities who are or will be determined to be in need of personal care or other supports that would allow them to remain in their homes and who select a spouse or parent to provide these services to them. Demonstration enrollees include the approximately 26,000 persons who were enrolled in the IHSS RP. The IHSS Plus benefits include:

- Self-directed, hands-on personal care services, which consist of the ability to hire, fire, and supervise personal caregivers, including spouses or parents; direction and management of caregivers' hours of service; and the choice to receive, in advance of services being rendered, the cash allotment to pay caregivers directly and hire substitute caregivers in urgent situations ("advance pay" option).

- Domestic and related services provided by a spouse or parent, i.e. house cleaning to reduce threats to participant health and safety; shopping for food and other necessities; miscellaneous chores; meal planning; preparation and clean-up; and routine laundry.
- Restaurant Meal Allowances (RMA), an option for participants whose disabilities prevent them from using their own cooking facilities and who are deemed to need RMA in lieu of meal planning, preparation, clean-up, and food shopping services that they would otherwise receive.
- Protective supervision by a spouse or parent, which consists of monitoring non self-directing persons, confused persons, or persons with mental illness by observing, reminding, cueing and/or redirecting participant behavior in order to safeguard the participant against injury, hazard, or accident.
- Up to 195 hours of assistance per month, or if service recipients have significant impairments, up to 283 hours per month.[29]

There are three types of service delivery modes:

- *Individual Provider Mode:* The participant directly hires, fires, and supervises an individual provider

- *Contract Mode:* The County or Public Authority enters into a contract with a third party, e.g., a home health agency, that provides a pool of workers

- *Homemaker Mode:* The County trains and employs individuals that provide personal care assistance.[30] The program will be operated at the county level.

Counties are responsible for:

- Processing applications for services
- Completing assessments of recipient needs for service
- Authorizing service hours based on the assessments

- Providing social worker assistance
- Receiving timesheets from providers and entering data into the payroll system
- Responding to consumer issues and complaints[31]

The California Department of Social Services is the "payroll agent" and as such will approve provider rates and calculate taxes, unemployment insurance, and workers' compensation benefits. Participants remain the "common law employer" of their service providers, but California law requires each of the state's 58 counties to act as the "employer of record" for collective bargaining purposes, or to establish a Public Authority, a Non-Profit Consortium, or a Joint Powers Agency to fulfill these duties. Most of the state's 58 counties have established a Public Authority.

The counties or these entities have the following responsibilities:

- Coordinate access to a provider chosen by the participant
- Maintain a provider registry to help find caregivers
- Conduct background checks
- Provide access to training for providers and participants
- Perform any other functions related to delivery of IHSS or RP services
- Ensure that all state and federal regulations are met[32]

No cost sharing is proposed. Participants could pay a share of cost for IHSS program services based on individuals' net non-exempt income in excess of the applicable SSI/SSP benefit level. There is no enrollment limit or cap on the number of people that can be enrolled.

The Department of Social Services Adult Programs Branch's Evaluation and Integrity Unit has ongoing quality assurance responsibilities, including conducting onsite reviews, investigating unusual events, and tracking consumer satisfaction and improvements by county. Public Authorities and the counties handle unusual events and emergencies that impact participants. County case managers are responsible for responding to participant issues or complaints. The State's Protection & Advocacy program; the State and Local Long-Term Care Ombudsman Programs; the Department of Mental Health; the Department of Developmental Services; the Office of Civil Rights in the Departments of Social Services and Health Services; the Area Offices for Aging; the Adult Protective Services system; and the Regional Centers are available to participants for advocacy support. The State plans to put in place additional quality assurance strategies during the demonstration.[33]

Conclusion

Waiver authority of the Social Security Administration and CMS offer states an immediate opportunity to be creative and innovative in their design of policies and procedures to promote individual self-sufficiency and community access and participation. The relationship between livable community principles and the goals of the HCBS wavier program are complementary. Individuals with disabilities across the age span are seeking ways to remain at home and in their community with public assistance to respond to their long-term support and service needs. Federal-state collaboration that takes maximum advantage of federal wavier authority offers a viable strategy to redesign the service delivery system to be responsive to changing consumer preferences and expectations to remain in and participate in community life.

Additional Resources

Florida Assisted Living http://www.floridaaffordableassistedliving.org

Florida Freedom Initiative Federal Register Notice: http://www.ssa.gov/regulations/articles/FL%20Freedom%20Initiative.htm

Memoranda: HCBS Quality Communication #10, 1915 (c) Waiver Application; Instructions and Technical Guide; Resource documents; CMS Review Instrument: November 15, 2005. Baltimore, Maryland: Centers for Medicare and Medicaid Services, Center for Medicaid and State Operations.

New Directions Waiver Fact Sheet. Maryland Developmental Disabilities Administration. http://www.tash.org/mdnewdirections/factsheets/index.htm

Maryland Developmental Disabilities Administration http://www.dda maryland.org/

Maryland Medicaid Website: Waiver Programs http://www.dhmh.state.md.us/mma/waiverprograms/

State Medicaid Agency Websites http://www.cms.gov/ medicaid/allState Contacts.asp

End Notes

[1] 42 U.S.C. § 1396.
[2] Schneider, A., Elisa, R., Garfield, R., et al. (2002) The Medicaid Resource Book. Menlo Park, CA: The Kaiser Commission on Medicaid and the Uninsured. Available at: http://www.kff.org/medicaid.
[3] *Understanding Medicaid Home and Community Based Services: A Primer* (2000) Washington DC: Office of the Assistant Secretary for Planning and Evaluation.
[4] Pub. L. No. 90-248, 81 Stat. 821 (1968).
[5] Omnibus Budget Reconciliation Act of 1981 (Pub. L. No. 97-35).
[6] Home and Community Based Services: Medicaid Research and Demonstration Waivers, Chart of State Participation (November 2004). Available at: http://www.pascenter.org/demo_waivers.
[7] Section 4442.5(B)(5) of the State Medicaid Manual.
[8] 42 CFR 440.
[9] Section 1902(a)(1) of the Social Security Act., 42 U.S.C. § 1396(a)(1).
[10] Section 1902(a)(10)(B) of the Social Security Act., 42 U.S.C. § 1396(a)(10)(B).
[11] http://new.cms.hhs.gov/IndependencePlus/
[12] Ibid.
[13] http://new.cms.hhs.gov/IndependencePlus/Downloads/IPFAQs.pdf
[14] Ibid.
[15] *New Hampshire* [§1915(c) new waiver, approved 12/16/02, effective 1/1/03]; *South Carolina* [§1915(c) new waiver, approved 3/11/03, effective 5/1/03]; *Louisiana* [§1915(c) new waiver, approved 4/24/03, effective 4/24/03]; *North Carolina* [§1915(c) new waiver, approved 12/23/03, effective 1/1/04] [§1915(b)/(c) new waiver, approved 10/6/04, effective 4/1/05]; *Florida* [§1115 amendment to Cash and Counseling, approved 5/30/03, effective 5/30/03]; *Maryland* [§1915(c) new waiver, approved 10/21/04, effective 7/1/05]; *California*[§ 1115 new demonstration, approved 7/30/04, effective 8/1/05]; *Delaware* [(§1915(b)/(c) new waiver, approved 11/12/04, effective 12/1/04]; *New Jersey* [§1115 amendment to Cash and Counseling, approved 12/15/04, effective date pending receipt of Operational Protocol]; *Connecticut* [§1915(c) new waiver, approved 1/14/05, effective 2/1/05].
[16] http://www.cms.hhs.gov/medicaid/1915c/
[17] U.S. General Accounting Office, Long Term Care, Federal Oversight of Growing Medicaid Home and Community Based Waivers Should Be Strengthened, Washington, June 2003.
[18] Effective January 1, 2007, States may cover HCBS services under the State plan for individuals with incomes below 150% of the federal poverty level ($1,225 a month for a one person household). Individuals are not required to meet the institutional level of need criteria as they must for 1915 (c) waivers.
[19] *New Directions Waiver Fact Sheet.* Maryland Developmental Disabilities Administration. Available at: http://www.tash.org/mdnewdirections/factsheets/index.htm
[20] Maryland has experienced a low participation rate as of this writing, but hopes that through improved marketing the program will have significant benefits for individuals with disabilities.
[21] Ibid.
[22] Maryland Developmental Disabilities Administration. Available at: http://www.ddamaryland.org/
[23] These may be part of an overall budget, but are not available for self direction.
[24] State of Florida, Agency for Persons with Disabilities (APD). Available at: http://apd.myflorida.com/2005-sc-handout-programs.htm#ffi
[25] Ibid.
[26] Ibid.

[27] *California Independence Plus Section 1115 Demonstration Fact Sheet*, December 1, 2004. http://www.cms.hhs.gov/medicaid/1115/ihssfs.pdf+California+In+Home+Supportive+Services+Plus+Demonstration+1115+&hl=en&start=1

[28] Ibid.

[29] Ibid.

[30] Ibid.

[31] Ibid.

[32] Ibid.

[33] Ibid.

In: Creating Livable Communities for People... ISBN: 978-1-60741-534-3
Editor: Alise Vanags

Chapter 8

RECOMMENDATIONS FOR ACTION

National Council on Disability

A livable community recognizes and responds to the universality of needs of its residents regardless of age, economic status, race, gender, or abilities. In improving its livability for one particular group of constituents, the community considers opportunities to respond to *all* community members' needs from a perspective of accessibility, equality, and inclusion.

This report identifies and highlights multiple strategies that may be applied to the design and support of livable community principles. The identified strategies have been initiated by federal and state government agencies as well as the private sector. These entities have recognized the power of collaboration and use of distinct tools to guide and stimulate systemic changes to make communities more livable for all. The highlighted strategies touch all facets of what livable communities do, that is provide residents with:

- Affordable, appropriate and accessible housing
- Affordable, accessible, reliable, and safe transportation
- Work and education opportunities
- Health and support services
- Civic, cultural, social, and recreational participation opportunities

The examples presented offer an optimistic view of the possibilities to change the way government organizes and manages resources, interacts with the business community and community developers, and responds to the expectations of evolving consumer interests, needs, and preferences for more choice and control in the delivery of support services.

Reviewing the six strategies presented in this report to promote more livable communities, NCD recognizes in the diverse approaches several common elements of design that support livable community objectives, such as the need to:

- Improve ease of access to and information about benefits, programs, and services for community members
- Stimulate private sector interest, involvement, and investment of resources through the use of tax incentives
- Consolidate program administration where appropriate and pool funds of multiple programs to improve consumers' ease of access to these programs
- Allow waivers of traditional rules of program eligibility, service architecture, and management of funds to improve coordination of public and private resources and consumer satisfaction
- Reach agreement on common performance measures across program authorities that recognize the value and benefits of the livable communities framework

The Council recognizes that to accelerate awareness and adoption of the highlighted strategies, there is no single recommendation that can produce the desired results at a community level. However, the following proposed recommendations offer multiple, complementary options for the legislative and executive branches of the Federal Government to direct needed attention to and proactively adopt strategies and policy levers that invest in livable community outcomes. With the aging of America and the challenges of disability in over 20 percent of families nationwide today, and possibly a greater percentage tomorrow, knowledge utilization and transfer from these best practices examples is essential.

RECOMMENDATIONS

1. **Issue a new Executive Order to charge the Office on Disability of the Department of Health and Human Services to chair a time-limited workgroup (six months, for example) on livable**

communities that includes representation by the Departments of Housing and Urban Development (HUD), Transportation, Education, Labor, Treasury, the Social Security Administration, the Centers for Medicare and Medicaid Services, the Administration on Aging, the Administration on Developmental Disabilities, and the Office of Community Services within the Department of Health and Human Services.

Implementation Lead: Office on Disability, HHS
The workgroup will identify policy barriers and facilitators for livable communities with particular emphasis on how to adopt and promote the use of the highlighted strategies in this report. Each agency will identify options for reduction of fragmentation in the service delivery system; improved coordination of access to services and benefits; expanded consumer choices and direction of services and supports; and development of strategic public and private partnerships that invest in livable community objectives, including universal design of housing, access to health care, transportation, education and employment, and cultural, social, and recreational opportunities. The final report to the President will include recommendations for policy and practice changes within each agency as well as in coordination with other agencies.

2. **Modify federal requirements for allocation of low-income housing tax credits so that, in making awards to developers, all states require a) the adoption of universal design standards, and b) documentation of approaches to allow a minimum of ten percent of units in multifamily affordable housing developments to be affordable to individuals with disabilities on fixed incomes (SSI/SSDI recipients).**

   Implementation Lead: Department of the Treasury, HUD
   The utilization of low income housing tax credits is one of the most significant financial resources still available to create affordable, safe, housing. The success of universal design standards adopted by the state of Kentucky, and required in all projects that are awarded tax credits to expand the availability of accessible living units, merits adoption at the federal level. The additional documentation regarding efforts to make a percentage of units affordable to individuals with

disabilities at 30 percent and below average median income would stimulate private investment in livable community objectives.

3. **Modify current performance measures being used to assess individual program strengths and weaknesses to focus on cross-department and agency collaboration to enhance livable community outcomes.**

Implementation Lead: Office of Management and Budget (OMB) The Program Assessment Rating Tool (PART) now being used by OMB has adopted common performance measures to evaluate programs and agencies across the Federal Government. However, there is no measure or analysis of cross-department and agency collaboration. There is also no adoption of the livable communities framework as the metric for measurement is on individual outcomes. Government agency and program performance should also focus on systems and system relationships. Three simple questions should be answered:

a. Is the program promoting livable community principles? (Provide documentation)
b. Through interagency and public-private strategic partnerships, is there improved ease of access to and information about coordinated programs, benefits, services, and supports that results in more livable communities? (provide documentation)
c. Are policies and procedures available, including waiver authority, to help communities more easily blend resources from multiple authorities to enhance livable community results with expanded consumer choice? (provide documentation)

An Annual Report to Congress should be prepared on individual agency performance.

4. **Utilize grant funds from the Centers for Medicare and Medicaid Services, Social Security Administration, and Departments of Labor, Commerce, Health and Human Services, Transportation, and Housing to offer a consolidated Livable Communities Program Initiative that streamlines 1) a single application for funds, 2) utilization of waiver authority, 3) consolidation of program management and service delivery, and 4) use of tax credits to reengineer the delivery of long-term supports,**

transportation, housing, employment, education, and cultural, social, and recreational opportunities at a community level.

Implementation Lead: Office on Disability, HHS
Collaborating Agencies: Domestic Policy Council; Administration on Aging; Department of Health and Human Services (HHS); Social Security Administration; Centers for Medicare and Medicaid Services
The unified grant initiative could support the more rapid evolution and demonstration of livable communities and move outside traditional silo funding of narrow areas of need to allow and stimulate more creative problem-solving.

5. **Expand tax incentives to promote matched savings plans for low-income wage earners across the life span.**

Implementation lead: Department of the Treasury; Senate Finance Committee; House Ways and Means Committee
Individual Development Accounts (IDAs) are promoting savings and asset development as a path to reduced dependency on government and improved self-sufficiency for low-income wage earners nationwide. To expand access to IDAs, an expanded tax incentive for financial institutions to match individual savings has been proposed and has received strong bipartisan support.
State and federally supported IDAs should be exempt from asset tests that determine continued eligibility for Social Security and Medicaid. The two authorizing Committees in the Senate and House should hold hearings on expansion of the IDA program to promote a better economic future for individuals with disabilities. The public-private sector partnership opportunity deserves the prompt attention of Congress as part of the livable communities framework.

6. **Utilize and leverage community service opportunities to create livable communities.**

Implementation Lead: Corporation for National Service (CNS)
The strength of a community can be defined by its inclusiveness and its accessibility. Americorps and VISTA members have engaged individuals of all ages in community service to improve safety and expand the quality of educational, employment, and recreational

opportunities. A Livable Community Initiative could target Americorps and VISTA volunteers to specific communities that can demonstrate a commitment to universal design elements to respond to the needs of all its residents. The focus of community service activities could include, but not be limited to, a range of challenges: affordable and accessible housing; social, cultural, and civic participation; access to lifelong learning; and improved transportation and health care systems. Awards of community service resources would be made on a competitive basis.

7. **Focus on the Gulf Coast recovery and rebuilding to promote livable community outcomes.**

   Implementation Lead: White House; Domestic Policy Council; Congress
   The reconstruction efforts in Louisiana, Mississippi, and Texas are in their early stages. There are many individuals with disabilities and seniors who have been displaced by the hurricanes. Multiple systems must be rebuilt, including, as priorities, housing, health care, and transportation. The area offers a unique opportunity to design with universal livability standards that promote the values of accessibility, equality, and inclusion. With the power of tax incentives and other federal resources, there is the opportunity to improve the quality of life for all individuals in the impacted region. By adopting universal design standards, individuals with disabilities should be a part of the decisionmaking process.

8. **Establish a National Resource Center on Livable Communities to educate policymakers, government administrators, community developers, people with disabilities, and the public about best practices in policy development and program implementation.**

   Implementation Lead: National Institute on Disability and Rehabilitation Research
   This report will help increase awareness of the growing number of examples of federal, state, and local action to respond to changing consumer expectations across the spectrum of age and disability. However, there is the need to establish a central source of information that continues to gather and update examples of communities that

have adopted and continue to improve the livability framework. There is the need for further research on the outcomes of new service architecture and the impact of increasing choice for consumers. The proposed Center should also be proactive in bringing diverse stakeholders together to enhance knowledge utilization.

APPENDIX A: MISSION OF THE NATIONAL COUNCIL ON DISABILITY

Overview and Purpose

The National Council on Disability (NCD) is an independent federal agency with 15 members appointed by the President of the United States and confirmed by the U.S. Senate. The purpose of NCD is to promote policies, programs, practices, and procedures that guarantee equal opportunity for all individuals with disabilities regardless of the nature or significance of the disability and to empower individuals with disabilities to achieve economic self-sufficiency, independent living, and inclusion and integration into all aspects of society.

Specific Duties

The current statutory mandate of NCD includes the following:

- Reviewing and evaluating, on a continuing basis, policies, programs, practices, and procedures concerning individuals with disabilities conducted or assisted by federal departments and agencies, including programs established or assisted under the Rehabilitation Act of 1973, as amended, or under the Developmental Disabilities Assistance and Bill of Rights Act, as well as all statutes and regulations pertaining to federal programs that assist such individuals with disabilities, to assess the effectiveness of such policies, programs, practices, procedures, statutes, and regulations in meeting the needs of individuals with disabilities.
- Reviewing and evaluating, on a continuing basis, new and emerging disability policy issues affecting individuals with disabilities in the

Federal Government, at the state and local government levels, and in the private sector, including the need for and coordination of adult services, access to personal assistance services, school reform efforts and the impact of such efforts on individuals with disabilities, access to health care, and policies that act as disincentives for individuals to seek and retain employment.

- Making recommendations to the President, Congress, the Secretary of Education, the director of the National Institute on Disability and Rehabilitation Research, and other officials of federal agencies about ways to better promote equal opportunity, economic self-sufficiency, independent living, and inclusion and integration into all aspects of society for Americans with disabilities.
- Providing Congress, on a continuing basis, with advice, recommendations, legislative proposals, and any additional information that NCD or Congress deems appropriate.
- Gathering information about the implementation, effectiveness, and impact of the Americans with Disabilities Act of 1990 (ADA) (42 U.S.C. § 12101 et seq.).
- Advising the President, Congress, the commissioner of the Rehabilitation Services Administration, the assistant secretary for Special Education and Rehabilitative Services within the Department of Education, and the director of the National Institute on Disability and Rehabilitation Research on the development of the programs to be carried out under the Rehabilitation Act of 1973, as amended.
- Providing advice to the commissioner of the Rehabilitation Services Administration with respect to the policies and conduct of the administration.
- Making recommendations to the director of the National Institute on Disability and Rehabilitation Research on ways to improve research, service, administration, and the collection, dissemination, and implementation of research findings affecting people with disabilities.
- Providing advice regarding priorities for the activities of the Interagency Disability Coordinating Council and reviewing the recommendations of this council for legislative and administrative changes to ensure that such recommendations are consistent with NCD's purpose of promoting the full integration, independence, and productivity of individuals with disabilities.
- Preparing and submitting to the President and Congress an annual report titled *National Disability Policy: A Progress Report.*

International

In 1995, NCD was designated by the Department of State to be the U.S. government's official contact point for disability issues. Specifically, NCD interacts with the special rapporteur of the United Nations Commission for Social Development on disability matters.

Consumers Served and Current Activities

Although many government agencies deal with issues and programs affecting people with disabilities, NCD is the only federal agency charged with addressing, analyzing, and making recommendations on issues of public policy that affect people with disabilities regardless of age, disability type, perceived employment potential, economic need, specific functional ability, veteran status, or other individual circumstance. NCD recognizes its unique opportunity to facilitate independent living, community integration, and employment opportunities for people with disabilities by ensuring an informed and coordinated approach to addressing the concerns of people with disabilities and eliminating barriers to their active participation in community and family life.

NCD plays a major role in developing disability policy in America. In fact, NCD originally proposed what eventually became ADA. NCD's present list of key issues includes improving personal assistance services, promoting health care reform, including students with disabilities in high-quality programs in typical neighborhood schools, promoting equal employment and community housing opportunities, monitoring the implementation of ADA, improving assistive technology, and ensuring that people with disabilities who are members of diverse cultures fully participate in society.

Statutory History

NCD was established in 1978 as an advisory board within the Department of Education (P.L. 95-602). The Rehabilitation Act Amendments of 1984 (P.L. 98-221) transformed NCD into an independent agency.

INDEX

D

E

I

Q

R

S

T

U

V

W

Y